WONDERCRUMP POETRY!

The best children's poems
from the third
Roald Dahl
Poetry Competition

Edited by Jennifer Curry

RED FOX

A Red Fox Book

Published by Random House Children's Books
20 Vauxhall Bridge Road, London SW1V 2SA

A division of Random House UK Ltd
London Melbourne Sydney Auckland
Johannesburg and agencies throughout the world

Copyright © Random House Children's Books 1996

1 3 5 7 9 10 8 6 4 2

First published in Great Britain by Red Fox 1996

Set in Janson by Fiona Webb, graphic designer

Printed and bound in Great Britain by
Cox & Wyman Ltd, Reading, Berkshire

Papers used by Random House UK Ltd are natural,
recyclable products made from wood grown in sustainable forests.
The manufacturing processes conform to the environmental regulations
of the country of origin.

RANDOM HOUSE UK Limited Reg. No. 954009

ISBN 0 09 968291 5

Contents

Introduction

It was a good year for poetry. We had our biggest entry yet. 15,000 poems were submitted, though sadly we can print only 160 of them. We discovered schools that had not sent us work before, as well as renewing acquaintance with those whose names are synonymous with excellent imaginative writing. We received more poems written by boys than we usually do. As a rule they are grossly outnumbered by the girls. And all the judges were conscious that the general mood of the poets was markedly more up-beat, optimistic and often funny.

The one major focus for writers' disappointment and grief was love in all its forms. Many poems told of unhappy friendships and love affairs, like Fabiola Smolowik's elegant elegy *The Twilight* – 'You should have stayed for the twilight/ If not for me', or Francesca Platt's angry shout – 'Old lover, dead meat'.

Of course, there was, as always, justifiable outrage at the condition of the world. Young Ellen Coffey, published for the third year running, summed up the general picture in *The Collector* – 'The faces of the hungry,/ The ruins of bombed houses,/ Dirty, crowded hospitals,/ The way they chop down forests./ I don't choose to collect these things./ They just jump into my mind.' Morgan Price was more specific in his lament for Shetland in the wake of yet another oil-spill disaster – 'On the tar-covered sand/ a seal is wriggling/ like a worm chopped in half.' Catherine McAleese tackled HIV in a mature and compassionate way and there was a heart-felt poem from Joanna Bell about

Alzheimer's Disease.

But there were less protest poems than usual and more that celebrated the joy of life – a girl's delight in the wily beauty of a fox 'The colour of autumn gold'; a boy's enjoyment of his flip-flops, 'for feet that are born to be free'; and, with a few notable exceptions, a general and recurring enjoyment of family life, 'Grandma is a sparkler/Grandad is golden rain'.

All the judges were delighted by the work of our Poet of the Year, Nancy Groves, especially her excellent *The Six Bridges* which managed to encapsulate the whole of life in six well-considered and crafted stanzas. And we were also unanimous in our choice of Mowden School, Hove, as the School of the Year and the Maharishi School, Ormskirk, as the winner of the Wondercrump Poetry Award. The quality of their original submissions, their variety, breadth and originality, made them both outstanding.

Congratulations to those of you who have won awards and those who have had your work printed here for all to read. Congratulations and thanks to all the others who made a real effort but didn't quite get through to the final 160. We do carefully read, consider and *value* your work even though we may not have sufficient pages to print it all and are immensely grateful to you for trying. Here's wishing you all more pleasure in poetry in the years ahead.

Jennifer Curry – Chair of the Judging Panel
Wondercrump Winners

Wondercrump Winners

Poet of the Year
Nancy Groves
Wimbledon High School
Wimbledon, London

School of the Year
Mowden School
Hove, East Sussex

Wondercrump Poetry Award
Maharishi School
Ormskirk, Lancashire

Age Category Winners
Age 7 and under
Jennifer Miles
Red Hill CE Primary School
Ellen Coffey
Handford Hall CP, Ipswich, Suffolk
Toni Mott
Handford Hall CP, Ipswich, Suffolk
Terry Baylis
Binfield C of E Primary School, Bracknell, Berkshire
Bradley Jennings
Howard Road School, Shanklin, Isle of Wight
Kelly Haylett
Townhill Junior School, Southampton, Hampshire

Age 8-11
Lisa Shovelar
Townhill Junior School, Southampton, Hampshire

Luke Yates

Maharishi School, Ormskirk, Lancashire

Jonathan Napier

Mowden School, Hove, East Sussex

Claire Salama

Darell Primary School, Richmond Upon Thames, London

Age 12-14

Rebecca Richardson

The Gregg School, Southampton, Hampshire

Rebecca Youens

Dr Challoner's High School, Little Chalfont, Buckinghamshire

Tessa Hart

Halesworth Middle School, Halesworth, Suffolk

Gordon Cullingford

Halesworth Middle School, Halesworth, Suffolk

Jessica Huth

Port Regis School, Shaftesbury, Dorset

James McLintock

Wisbech, Cambridgeshire

Age 15-17

Stephen John

Porthcawl Comprehensive School, Porthcawl, Mid Glamorgan

Timothy Watts

The Holy Trinity School, Crawley, West Sussex

Francesca Platt

Canon Slade School, Bolton, Lancashire

Catharine McAleese

Ripon Grammar School, Ripon, North Yorkshire

Fabiola Smolowik

Forest (Girls') School, Snaresbrook, London

Eva Okwonga

West Drayton, Middlesex

The
Roald Dahl
Foundation

Throughout his life, Roald Dahl gave of his time and money to help people in need. When he died, his widow, Felicity Dahl, established The Roald Dahl Foundation to continue this generous tradition. The Foundation's aim is to serve people in the UK in three major areas:

- **Literacy**, because it was Roald's crusade. Literacy is the most basic educational tool . It is also the passport to hours of pleasure. For many reasons, some people and some groups need extra help to help them to achieve this essential skill. The Foundation offers grants to a diverse group in this arena.

- **Neurology**, because brain damage has severely affected the Dahl family. Neurology funds specialise in the areas of epilepsy and head injury. In addition to our ongoing programme of individual grants to people in financial hardship, the Foundation grants funds to specially identified projects.

- **Haematology**, because leukaemia was the cause of Roald's death. Our haematology grants target areas where funds are particularly hard to come by, but where the need in undeniably great. IN addition to many individual grants, the Foundation supports large-scale projects.

All monies donated to the Foundation are directed where they are required – to people in the UK with specific needs. If you would like to know more about us, or help the Foundation in its work by making a donation then please write to us direct:

The Roald Dahl Foundation
92 High Street Great Missenden
Buckinghamshire HP16 0AN
England

THE
FUTURE
OOZES OUT

You're a Miracle

You're a perfect creature
Sealed safely in a womb
Completely unknown.
Who will you be?
How will you smile?
What will make you cry?
Innocent and new,
You're pure and helpless,
What treats you have in store.
You've never heard the sea crashing on the rocks.
Nor smelled the flowers in spring.
You've never felt the sun shining on your face.
Nor seen your mum's soft smile.
You're silent.
You're patient.
You're waiting,
For the door of life to open.

Hannah Magor (10)
Lowes Wong Junior School
Southwell, Nottinghamshire

Myself Meets I

In my dream I turn to see,
A small familiar girl
Run up to me.
Myself looks up,
And I look down,
Present into past,
Past into now.
Our brown eyes meet.
Identical.
We silently greet.
She turns and runs away
Back into yesterday.
Did she approve
Of what she saw of herself,
As I am now?

Helen Reed (13)
Andover, Hampshire

My Future

Half an hour to go
Will he be on time?
No, that's not his car.
What if he's late?
Don't bite your nails John.
You promised yourself.
Is that him, no?
Yes – he's opening the gate.
Walking up the drive.
My heart beat is rising.
I'm shivering all over.
He pushes it through.
That brown envelope lies on the mat.
A shaking hand lifts it up,
I slit open its throat.
The future oozes out.

John Boucher (10)
St. Brigid's Primary School
Derry, N. Ireland

Glass Cups

Two, dressed in little flowery dresses,
One other dressed in dungarees and a T-shirt.
They came in from the garden,
Into the kitchen, just like old people.
'Can we have a drink, Grandma?' they shouted.
'Yes, if you say please,' Gran said to my cousins.
She lifted the plastic cups down from the shelves.
'We want glass ones like you, Grandma,' they said.
'No, you might drop them,' said Gran.
As they drank, it reminded me of old people.
One day they will be glad of plastic cups,
When they're old,
Frail in every movement.
And when their children's children
Want glass cups,
They will think back to the time
When they were young and wanted to be old,
With all the confidence of real cups.

Esme Trussler (13)
Halesworth Middle School,
Halesworth, Suffolk

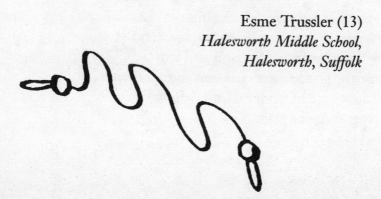

The six Bridges ___

When I was young, I built a bridge of adventure.
It stretched to the sun and back,
Suspended between silver moons and distant planets.
It was made of mystery and imagination.
Underneath sailed galleons swarming with pirates,
Dragons circled overhead, mermaids beckoned,
And a brave knight in gleaming armour
Galloped across to save the princess with the long shining
  hair.

When I was growing up, I built a bridge of dreams.
It circled the world, a thing of great beauty.
A river of happiness flowed beneath its arches,
Anxiety eddied between its piers.
It was made of secrets and uncertainties,
Its foundations rested on shadows,
But its towers reached to the stars.

When I was grown, I built a bridge of love.
It joined and embraced, closing the chasm.
As warm as sleep and as strong as devotion,
It was woven from affection and trust,
Knotted together with passion and tenderness.
It sang to me of gladness and delight;
It sang to me of pain.

When I was getting old, I built a bridge of fear.
It crossed my days and divided my nights.
It was as cold as suspicion,
As treacherous as quicksand.
It trembled over the void,
Supported by pillars of despair and loneliness,
Grounded in fatigue.

When I was old, I built a bridge of memories.
It spanned a life.
It was made of laughter and tears,
Of sadness and joy.
It was the connection that held everything together.
It reached backwards and forwards in time
But its approaches were shrouded in mist.

Now I am dying, I have built a bridge of hope.
Its golden path leads forward to eternity.
Above, the sky is a clear blue arch;
Below, the world is slowly turning.
I am at peace.

Nancy Groves (13)
Wimbledon High School,
Wimbledon, London
(Poet of the Year)

When I Am Old

When I am old, don't expect me to like it.
No big comfy cardigans for me.
No sensible shoes and no wrinkled stockings.

When I am old, I won't do crosswords.
No knitting needles that click and clack.
No shawls down my bent old back.

When l am old, I shall have a cat,
to keep me company
to sit with me on my lap.

When I am old, don't expect me to enjoy it.
I'll get a horrible cough,
and see the doctor every day.

When I am old and my legs won't work
and my shoulders feel sore,
I hope that someone will come to my door.

When I am old I'll take my teeth out at night,
And hang my wig on the chair,
And then I'll dream that I'm young again.

Amelia Clarke (12)
Sir William Robertson High School
Welbourn, Lincolnshire

My Final Resting Place

When I die, put me in a coffin made of cardboard so that it will not last forever.

Plant an oak tree on top of me and watch it grow tall and strong.

It will be my tree, my final resting place.

Although my body may be dead, I will live on through my tree in every branch, every acorn.

I will feed it with my soul and my spirit it will hold.

Fiona Gordon (13)
St Aloysius College,
Garnethill, Scotland

I Remember

I remember
That there was a little girl
When I was two
She screamed and played
My ears nearly drowned
Then I grew up
I remember when I was two.

Stacey Kemp (7)
Toftwood First School
Dereham, Norfolk

The Gouffre*

In time frozen, the falling spears hang,
Lion's fangs, from which you must escape,
You have a million years,
To marvel at the slowed-down world.
Lives pass above, spanning a length so short,
When charted not measurable,
On this primordial masterpiece,
Each generation as insignificant as the last.
For some the work is over,
In a slow-motion collision, they meet,
The impact crushes, thickening them as it dispels,
Joined now they stand, mighty pillars,
Towers of time.
As each millennium goes by,
The cavern is portioned off, sold to darkness,
Steadily the gaps close, shutting down,
This subterranean world.

*Gouffre – Chasm or cavern deep underground

Cameron Queen (13)
Blairgowrie, Perthshire

SLOWLY AS A SNAIL

Clock

Hours pass
Slowly as a snail
Creeping between the grass blades
Of the minute

Rebecca Wilkinson (10)
Bulwell St. Mary's Primary School
Bulwell, Nottingham

Night

Sometimes
I think
my mum's coat
is a person burgling
us.

Iceni Elmer (7)
St Peter's Primary School
Henfield, West Sussex

So Quiet

It's so, so quiet in my bed, in my bed,
As the thoughts of the day settle down in my head.
I listen to the silence and the noises that I hear,
Are the noises that are usually too quiet for my ear.

I hear the tiny tiptoe of a mouse softly creeping,
And the bustle and the rustle of a spider weaving.
I hear the flutter of a bird in flight,
And the whoosh of a meteor as it whizzes through the
   night.
I listen to the creaking of a moth's jewelled wing,
My ear tunes in when the crickets start to sing.
I hear the shrill-pitched squeaking of a swooping bat,
And the cautious patter of a sneaking cat.
I hear the splishing splatter of the tumbling rain,
And the snuffling of a badger lumbering home again.
I hear the noises of a house, fast asleep,
I hear a ghost when the floorboards creak!

It's so, so quiet in my bed, in my bed.
The thoughts of the day have settled down in my head
I have listened to the silence and the noises that I've heard
Are the noises of nature in a dark and peaceful world!

Katharine Jones (8)
Weymouth, Dorset

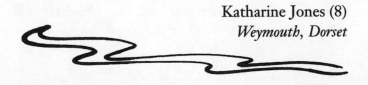

I Hate Alarm Clocks

You know, alarm clocks are made to disturb you from your
beauty sleep before you need to wake up?
That means that they are designed to wreck your life!

Alarm clocks are there to make you force your long eye-
    lashes apart and
as if that's not enough torture for one morning,
grasp the energy from nowhere to
swing an arm in the effort to stop the noise.

It can't be healthy! It really can't!

Some people roll over and go back to sleep.
Some mutter, 'Great, is it morning already? It can't be! Oh
    no!'

Then it literally dawns upon you.

'Sheesh. I have to move. I've got a million things to get
done before work,'
sigh the busy people, minds clicking into action for the day
ahead.

Some (the tired, weary people) prise open their eyelids and
look gloomily into their mirrors, only to horrify
themselves with the sight of their reflections:-

Dark circles, wrinkles or bags under their eyes, swollen
    faces, bed hair,
hoarse voices from screaming during scary nightmares,
stubbly cheeks, spots from make-up not removed the
    previous night,
bruises turning purple from a big fight,
slow movements, bad breath, troubled spirits, smelly
    underarms,
feeling woozy because of excess alcohol swimming in the
    bloodstream
from the night before,
Sometimes you think you can take it no more,
a stiff neck, other aches and pains, creases on skin,
your nose looks bigger, you're more fat, less thin,
lights and/or radio left on, homework not done,
sheets on the floor,
the bed's not even dry anymore (the hot-water bottle had
    leaked)
Crumpled work shirts, eyes stinging madly as you absent-
    mindedly left in
your contacts, so you're feeling dead,
– Not surprising, the cat slept on your head . . .

Need I go on . . .? Does any of the above sound like you?

All the worries come flooding back,
when you notice the running tap . . .

You pull on your dressing gown, with gravy on it from
    Sunday dinner
(Yesterday you didn't get dressed)

However . . .
Some bright, rare, energetic madmen awake
like a red-eyed gerbil . . . Up all day, up all night . . . not
    tired,
full of optimism and anticipation for the next twenty-four
    hours.
'Time for a good run around the block and a bowl of
    Kellogg's Bran Flakes!'
Heck, you might even do Mr Motivator's workout too!

But don't you just hate having to wake at
the shrill ring of a stupid machine?
After all – you're really not keen
to go to school or work.

Alarm clocks.
They run and ruin your life.
And they're here to stay.

I HATE ALARM CLOCKS!!

But another day has arrived –
Ready
Or not.

Helen Criddle (15)
Cardiff High School,
Cardiff

All in a Minute

The golden globe rises over the silky sands
Of a desolate, tropical island

A drunken, old beggar slumps down
Against a decrepit graffiti-covered wall

A teenaged party animal raves on
As the night wears old

A middle-aged gambler
Loses his life savings at the turn of a card

A prominent rock star dashes onto stage
Before thousands of adoring fans

A hunger-stricken infant wails for attention
To no avail

A chorus of monotonous cats
Continues into the night

A jubilant busker plays a joyful tune
Without a worry in the world

A large, African elephant is shot down
By a group of vicious poachers with ivory on their mind
And so passes another minute.

Mark Mulvihill (13)
Riverston School
London

A Waking City

Gently, I ease my bedroom window – up,
up towards the sleeping sky.
All that can be seen,
Obscuring mist enveloping the city
like a grey duvet,
Towering skyscrapers
peep from under the covers.
But the sun rises early,
working hard to lift that duvet,
and to wake the dormant city.
The early mist;
a natural sieve,
filters the precious beams of morning light.
The sky; an artist's canvas
on which fresh paint drips down; a flowing river.
Up ahead
Old Tower Bridge,
A venerable titan in the morning air,
Holds up the sky
like a sentry, guarding safe passage,
letting wandering ships drift,
under its tired, ample frame.
Below
Traffic is building up,
until cars mingle;
a pack of wolves, /
snarl away from the lights.

Above
sluggish clouds,
ride their monotonous journey
across the earth,
to shadow the land.
While up on high,
the sun secretly slips
through the dispersing mist,
and
silhouettes of silent houses
emerge
as the city wakes . . .

Jamie Thomson
Mowden School (12)
Hove, East Sussex
(School of the Year)

A Whole Night

A Whole Night
To sleep
A Whole Night
To pray
A Whole Night
To dream
A Whole Night
To stray
It's a new world.

A Whole Night
To feast
A Whole Night
To think
And A Whole Night
To change into a
fierce beast.

Shasa Emtage (7)
St Cedd's School
Chelmsford, Essex

FAMILY
FIREWORK
SHOW

Family Noises

Mums scream.
Dads shout.
Brothers stamp
And jump about.
Sisters whine
With all their might.
Babies gurgle
With delight.

Anna Fenton (8)
Hall Green Junior School
Birmingham

Hard Work

Is it up or is it down or is it over?
I wish my mum would buy slip-on shoes.
Is it up or is it down or is it over?

Bradley Jennings (6)
Howard Road School
Shanklin, Isle of Wight
(Age Category Winner)

Why do the Clouds Fly?

Go on it's bed time
Dad why do the clouds fly?
Um they're tied on string and held up by gods
How do the gods get up there?
Um they get up there on ladders
How big are the ladders?
Um 2000 metres high
How long is that Dad?
It's time for bed
How long is the night, Dad?

Jennifer Miles (7)
Red Hill CE Primary School
Worcester
(Age Category Winner)

Georgie

My sister is pretty
She likes to chew her toes
She has light hair
She runs around a lot.
I have to follow her.
She pretends she's a monkey
I think she's a cheetah.

Hannah Watkins (5)
Barnsbury Infant School
Woking, Surrey

Dentist

What I hate,
About going to the Dentist,
Is the waiting room,
Silent
Until someone screams behind a wall.

What I hate,
About going to the Dentist,
Is the smell of hygiene in the room,
And the chair squeaks as you sit down.

What I hate,
About going to the Dentist,
Is the chair moving,
Sounding like a factory,
And the blinding light, cast down in your eyes.

What I hate,
About going to the Dentist,
Is your mouth being stretched into an oblong,
The picking of the plaque,
And the scraping of teeth.

What I hate,
About going to the Dentist,
Is the drill that touches your teeth,
And makes your mouth shake,

Like a pneumatic drill on a road,
The vibrations like music on full blast.

What I hate,
About going to the Dentist,
Is the sharp injection of pain,
The hurt as the needle goes in,
That numbs your mouth,
That wobbles your tongue and lips,
Like jelly as you try to speak.

What I hate,
About going to the Dentist,
Is the slimy pink liquid,
The swallow and the spit.

What I like,
About going to the Dentist,
Is being given a sticker,
Being made a fuss of by Mum,
And watching my brother go in next!

Karina Bailey (9)
Mereway Middle School
Mereway, Northampton

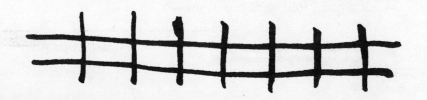

The World in My Room

An angry rhino, my mum
Enters my room like a hurricane,
Yelling in a voice as loud as a railway engine,
'Tidy your room or it will be the worse for you!'
She towers over me, hands on hips, looking like Goliath.
So, wearily, I get out the cleaning implements
And begin to polish inevitably.

Duster swirling round the table like a grand lady
Dressed in chiffon to a lordly ball,
Her gown cleaning a path through Tableland.

Hoover eating dust, gorging itself
On my bedroom floor.Suddenly, as I slip it under my bed,
It splutters and dies,
Choking on a discarded sock.

Books falling into line under my hand
Like soldiers in an army regiment.
I am the sergeant, sternly commanding them.
I imagine myself with a whistle round my neck,
In army clothes presiding over the rest.
Suddenly the terrifying major storms in and . . .
'What a good job!' says my mum.

Helen Mort (9)
Calow, Chesterfield

Washing Up

Soapy Bubbles that squelch and squirm
A big bowl of water, wet and warm
Squeaky dishes that slide and slip
It's not so bad when you get into it!

With sleeves rolled up and bubbles galore
A rainbow wonderland in every tiny mirror ball
Reflecting a hundred matching faces
Shiny tea cups, silver spoons and empty spaces.

If you cup your hands and blow them high
Into the air they'll dance and fly
Until the glistening pops and silently disappears
Leaving fingers wrinkled soft and wet, and then,
'Are those dishes all washed up yet?'

Sarah Gunn (10)
Kirkburton Middle School
Huddersfield, West Yorkshire

The Kitchen's Going Crazy

The taps keep dripping
The pipes have sprung a leak
There's no water for the dishwasher
There's no washing for a week.

The saucepan lids keep rattling
The cutlery's got the shakes
The carving knife keeps buzzing
The oven won't bake the cakes.

The microwave keeps pinging
The light goes on and off
The kettle keeps on boiling
And that's with them both turned off.

The cupboard doors all clatter
The shelves jump up and down
With packets, jars and tins and things
My mum's brought home from town.

The fridge and freezer are getting hot
I think they've blown a fuse
The iron hisses smoke not steam
There's nothing safe to use.

The kitchen is at war with us
I can't have my favourite gravy
It isn't safe to go in there
The kitchen's going crazy.

Alastair Norman (11)
Sir William Robertson High School,
Welbourn, Lincolnshire

When I'm On My Own

When I'm on my own,
I feel cold
like a block of ice.
But
when I have a hug
from my mum
I melt.

Alice Aldous (8)
Darell School
Richmond, Surrey

The World Inside My Fridge

The fridge hums in time with the rain
Splattering on the window.
Tacky magnets arranged inartistically on the door.
Inside the dull light casts shadows,
Of last night's pizza,
And a newly-opened packet of salmon spread.
The mouldy yoghurts sit at the back,
Infested with germs,
Over-populating the fridge.
Cling-film covered sweetcorn stares with hostility,
At the minced beef.

The over-packaged food fills each shelf,
Greens and reds brightening the sterile walls.
Beer bottles lined up like soldiers,
Standing to attention as the milk carton
Inspects their silver-label uniforms.
The old aura of the fridge fills the room,
Hairs on backs of necks stand up,
And toes curl inside soft white trainers.
Flies buzz around the room,
But never dare to invade the fridge.
The door closes and the light is put out.

The room a little less bright,
But a little warmer,
Returns to normal.

The darkness inside the fridge,
Acts like morphine,
Inducing calmness.
The sweetcorn makes its peace with the minced beef,
And the beer-bottle soldiers,
March in time,
To the familiar hum,
Of the fridge.

Alix Martin (15)
Umberleigh, North Devon

Murder!

I stand, knife in both hands,
I grip the handle, fiercely.
There it is, alone on the table,
A world away from others of its own kind.

It sits, still on a cloth,
I wonder,
How should I do this,
Slowly or quickly?

I raise my arms,
And close my eyes
As I bring down the knife
Making a loud thud.

I slowly open my eyes,
And look down at the table
As a tear falls from my eye.
Lying there, cut in half –
The onion.

Claire Morton (14)
Duchess's High School
Alnwick, Northumberland

Leaving Home

Why, Mum why?
Why do you leave me?
Your last words are all I will have.
In my home I will be loved,
In my home I will be cared for.
Out there, what will happen to me?

The warmth of her body, soft and loving,
How long have I got to wait?
One last word and one more loving kiss,
One last smell of your sweet perfume,
One last moment for us to be together.
How long will the war go on?

'Don't forget your manners'
Comes a voice.
A red face and a quivering lip,
Blinking eyes, trying not to cry,
Prickling eyes and a sandpaper throat.
Run to the train, don't let her see me.

The train starts up, with me at the window
Peering out, everything starts to blur
As the train moves away you start to get smaller,
'Bye Mum, goodbye, I'll never forget you.'
I will always have the faded memories,
Of you.

Sarah Carman (10)
Winterbourne Senior Girls' School
Thornton Heath, Surrey

The Empty House

I open the door
It creaks,
It groans
I step inside
The house feels unwelcoming
I switch on the light
It clicks
It flickers on and off for a second or more
I go into the living room
It seems strange without anybody there
I touch some familiar objects
I hear a noise on the landing
It was creaking
Slowly I make my way up the stairs
My shadow startles me at first
I hear a noise behind me
I freeze for a second or two
I dash forward into my room
I scramble into bed
Hide myself under the blankets
A minute later I peep out
Phew!
It was only the cat.
I slowly make my way down stairs

Snuggle up in my favourite armchair
Making me safe for the time being
Wishing my mum would come home to comfort me.

Richard Webber (10)
Deansfield Junior School
Eltham, London

Mum said

Whodoyouthinkyouare?
Your daughter I've been here for nearly thirteen years.
TALK to me with some respect, RESPECT!
I just walked . . . . . off.
Do . . . . your . . . homework.
Ididn'tgetanytoday I bellowed down the stairs.
CLEAN up that bedroom.
It's clean.
Shut . . . . the . . . . door.
I should get paid for the amount of times I do this I thought.
Do . . . . as . . . . you're . . . . . told for once, JUST ONCE!
You'renotgoingoutlookinglikethat.
When you look perfect you may criticise.
Whileyou'reundermyroof . . . . you . . . . do . . . as . . I . . . say.
I'll go out and do as I please then, I was about to say.
But I just bit . . . . my . . . lip . . . and . . . walked . . . . AWAY.

Vicky Pomroy (12)
Rainham School for Girls
Gillingham, Kent

My Dad Says

I say
I want to go to Burger King for some chips
He says
You can't have chips
You have to go to Chip King.
He says
Don't sleep with your mouth open under the pillow
Or you will wake up with a mouth full of money.
I say
I'm bored
He says
What cardboard, blackboard or whiteboard.
I say
I'm hungry
He says
I'm Lesley.
He says
It's better to be fat and happy
Than skinny and wretched.
He has a lot to say
Does my Dad.

William Grihault (8)
Wheatley Primary School
Wheatley, Oxford

Parents

Parents are telephones,
Constantly interrupting.
Uncomfortable silences.
Continuous, critical, persistent, provocative.
Faulty or efficient,
No telling what you'll hear next.
Parents are telephones, constantly interrupting.

Parents are signposts at the crossroads,
Guiding you onto the right road.
Helpful, yet sometimes unreadable.
Vague about direction, certain about destination.
Showing you the best route.
Parents are signposts at the crossroads,
Guiding you onto the right road.

Parents are promises,
Vows that will never be broken.
Given before you are born,
Kept until you die.
Declarations of trust.
Parents are promises,
Vows that will never be broken.

Jenny Clough (14)
John Taylor High School,
Burton-upon-Trent, Staffordshire

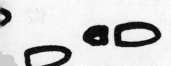

Parents

As children we look up to them
We idolise and adore them
They are our heroes and protectors
They built the world we live in
They are our role models.

As teenagers we sneer at them
We ignore and belittle them
They are our jailers and persecutors
They are our enemies.

As we grow up we become them.

Siân Lambert (16)
Hoveringham, Nottinghamshire

Blind with Loss of a Nanny

Blind with uncertainty, I have watched
My Nanny, as she sits sewing dresses,
That attention-stealing activity which fills up her days,
Her face crumpled up, like some
Used-up old masterpiece, too loved to be thrown away.
Her hands, swollen up like sausages, absorbed in their
Work, and yet apart from it in mind, with a haunting
Mist of weakness which clouds over her, making me
Hazy and uneasy as a swallow before its first flight,

Knowing that times will come, but being
Swept into a whirling cyclone of love,
Dizziness and forgetfulness with her

Blind with horror, having reality smothered into our faces
We strangle through the days; we can but face the truth.
She has strayed from her hospital, wandering,
With no indication of home, no indication of where
She belongs, only as far as the neighbour's home.
Does home mean so little to her?
We have to collect her, and then she lies there, a human
In body but deformed in mind, lingering on with
Sickening sweetness and love and I almost
Want her to . . . but I can't bring myself to say that.

Blind with loss, I am forced to remember her
Last moments, the loving cruelty of feeding her with a
Plastic spoon and beaker.
Then those sickening words of hope
'We'll see what the morning brings.' And then the morning
Brings its fatal gift. The pure irony of wanting
Death and yet fearing it. The hatred of hearing
People say, 'So sorry to hear about your Nanny, you
Must be terribly upset.' Then the terror of seeing my
Own mother, sewing, resembling Nanny, and
Knowing that I cannot say any more, for
There is no more to say.

Joanna Bell (14)
Ashton, Avon

Grandad

Grandad sits,
Smothered in the folds of his favourite chair,
Dozing by the fire.
His wrinkled-up paper bag of a face
Lights up with joy
As we pile through the door for a visit.
He seems dozy
A sleepy old cat,
But he's really got a supersonically sharp brain,
Hidden in many years of ageing.
He's a living encyclopedia of stories and facts
Lost in the mists of time.
When we leave,
He snuggles down,
And is once again swallowed by his armchair.

Neville Doyle (11)
Mowden School,
Hove, East Sussex
(School of the Year)

Grandpa

My grandpa lived in black and white.
He woke to a monochrome sunrise,
Turned on the wireless,
And listened to sombre words
About black and white planes
Dropping raven bombs.

Grandpa's clothes were made frosted and sooty,
By the stern wind
That tousled his dark hair
Above a pallid face.

He would walk down a dull street
And catch the black and white smell
Of white fish in batter
Wrapped in black and white paper.

He'd sit on the pier,
A huge ebony structure,
With a quicksilver sea below,
Where snow swans swayed
And watched him with plastic-bead eyes

Until the heavy sky turned blacker still
And tiny white stars blinked again
In that world of lead.

Zoe Layton (15)
Longview School,
Colchester, Essex

Curtains

'Hello?'
You call me from behind your curtain.
'I could hear you ask for me,' you say.
I got the highest English mark in my year, Grandad.
And your face lights up.

You sigh,
You close your eyes and you sleep.
I want to hear your stories,
Tell me things to make me miss you.
And deep down I dread that you will.

I giggle at your jokes,
And you at mine.
'They're moving me tomorrow,' you say.
I think I flinch.
'I'll be more comfortable, though,
And they have squirrels.'

Grandad?
New place, same curtains.
'I think I'll like it here,' you say.
You open your hand, 'a watch for you to watch.'
'And think of me,' you forget to add.
And our faces light up.

Eve Kennedy (17)
Canon Slade School
Bolton, Lancashire

The Family Portrait

Staring at the family portrait I was thinking of the
Happiness that there used to be,
Gran always sat on the edge,
She insisted on it being that way,
With Mum in the middle and Dad sitting next to her,
Always in the living room never in the kitchen,
Little Tom sat at the front in his little blue sailor outfit,
And Sarah Jane in her best frock with a bow in her hair,
And Charles is right at the back,
Always in the living room, never in the kitchen.

Now Gran sits in her rocking chair deserted,
Mum sits in a small flat in Leeds listening to the silence;
Dad lives in London in showbusiness by himself,
Not-so-little Tom is in College lonely,
But poor Sarah Jane died two years ago,
And Charles, well he has a job at a takeaway in Wales.
All alone.

Helen Burden (10)
Kirkburton Middle School
Huddersfield, West Yorkshire

Seeing All My Family

Seeing all my family
together
at special occasions.
Is a brilliant firework show
going off.

Grandma is a sparkler,
Grandad is golden rain
making us brighter.
My cousins
are Catherine Wheels.
My dad is a banger
because he always talks too loud.
The best one of all
that lights up the sky
so everyone stares
is my mum
the incredible blast of sparkle
the rocket.

Every time we meet,
It always has the same effect
our family firework show.

Claire Salama (10)
Darell Primary School
Richmond Upon Thames, London
(Age Category Winner)

MIX IN 30-ODD CHILDREN

Classroom Creation

Start with a reasonable sized room.
Add a dozen oblong tables,
Each with six chairs.
Drop in an intelligent teacher,
And sprinkle on some excellent work.
Mix in thirty-odd children
(A mixture of friendly girls and fussy boys).
Blend in good behaviour.
Warm it, making sure that it is immensely comfy.
Fill in the spaces with a carpet,
And don't forget the blackboard,
Along with dusty chalks,
And a clean cloth.
Make it full of happiness and joy.
Add a wooden door and glass windows.
Cover with a horizontal roof,
And some electric lights.
Fix in shelves with paperback books on.
Place a playground outside.
Fill it with oxygen and
Your fresh classroom is FINISHED!
And ready for use.

Natalie Harnett (9)
Crossways Junior School
Thornbury, Avon

I Remember

I remember when I was young and
didn't go to school.
I felt nice and cosy at home.
I liked having hugs from Mummy.
My sisters were younger than me.
Daddy had to go to work.
Now I have to go to school and it's
not cosy any more.

Esther Jones (6)
Neston CP School
Neston, Wilts.

Creases

Creases like knives down the middle of trousers,
like a train track down the middle of my maths book.
Games kit lying on the floor
in a puddle of creases.
Faces crumpled with grief and faces crumpled with
   laughter.
Which do I like best?
Straight creases keep me in order,
Crumpled creases reflect my chaos.

Andrew Tucknott (10)
Yarm Preparatory School
Yarm, Cleveland

Maths Lesson

In a Maths lesson
Trying to work these questions out
I don't know how to add fractions
Persevering and persisting ...
It's impossible.

Mr Humphries is in the other corner
of the room ...
Minutes seem like hours trying to figure this out.

'All right then,' he says.
It falls silent.
Well, at least I don't have to go on doing this.

It's easy now ...
Just sit back and listen
Someone else will explain –
They always do.

'Right then,' he says,
'T O M I A K – what should I do to start off with?'

The words hit me like a bullet.
My throat goes dry.
Whispers go around the room.

I look around frantically,
'What do I do?'
Heartbeat pounding.
All eyes fixed on me.
Trying to get an answer from someone.
I've got to say something.

What can I say?
Tension ... Pressure.
'Erm, well ... I'm not actually too sure
how to do it, Sir ...'
WHAT ELSE could I have done?

Matthew Tomiak (12)
Worcester

The Wars of the Roses

Bored, I sat,
Glanced at the clock,
Another twenty-five minutes to endure.
How much is there to know about the Wars of the Roses,
     anyway?
A blue bottle buzzed angrily, trapped as I was.
Chalk dust hung heavy in the air.
'England was changing at the end of the fifteenth century.'
Who cares!
I fiddled with my compass,
Started to scratch at my desk, tagging my name.
Another entry in the dynastic line
Reaching back through years of apathetic schoolgirls.
'The English nobles were beginning to quarrel among
     themselves.'
My ruler fell to the floor. The teacher spun round,
Glared at me, irritated,
Then turned wearily back to the board.
I leant over.
A folded dart of paper flicked past my ear
Landed on my desk, stared up at me,
And I heard a hissed 'Read it'.
'Financially and morally bankrupt, the barons turned on one
     another.'
My attention caught at last, I read the note.
A tiny scrap of paper,
But the words burnt into me like acid;

No goggles or overall protected me.
The letter did not address me as 'Dear';
The hostile word 'To' preceded my name.
YOU'RE SO SAD.
AND YOU'RE REALLY BUGGING US.
SO, IF YOU DON'T MIND, WE'D RATHER NOT
   HAVE
ANYTHING MORE TO DO WITH YOU
   FROM ...
And then the names of my two best friends.
'Their wrangling turned into a civil war.'
In an instant everything had changed;
I dug my nails into my palms in a vain attempt
To hold back my tears of betrayal and fury.
I wanted to smash my fist into the two faces
I saw smirking at me from across the room
I wanted to run away and hide.
'We call that period the Wars of the Roses.
It lasted thirty years.'

I have never forgotten the Wars of the Roses.

Nancy Groves (12)
Wimbledon High School
Wimbledon, London
(Poet of the Year)

Great Expectations

Ma dad sez skool is
fer puffs.
E sez yool become a
wuss if thar goes.
Ma teacher sez I
don't know ma tables.
But ma dad sez tables
are fer eatin' off.
Arm gonna become a
Senior Flux Capacitor Engine
Design Co-ordinator.

Azizum Akhtar (14)
Kimberworth Comprehensive School
Rotherham

The Excuse

Riding through the night he came,
Black cape flying,
White horse shining,
Hands stretched out to reach me.

Sweat trickled down my face,
Hands trembling,
Teeth chattering,
The paper clutched to my chest.

The rain came down in rivers,
Thunder flashing,
Lightning rumbling,
Soaking the ground before me.

Closer and closer he came,
Heartbeat pounding,
Blood rushing,
As he snatched the paper from me.

So you must understand, Sir,
My homework is done,
But, carelessly,
I let it be stolen by the
man from the night.

Kate Flynn (13)
St Bede's School
Redhill, Surrey

Trouble

I walked quickly to the office,
Past lots of giggling boys.
My heart was thudding like a clock,
My tummy made a noise.
An angry Mr Dover,
Marched sternly to my side.
Whatever will he say to me?
I very nearly cried.
Mrs Locock stood behind me,
So quiet and so strict.
I felt her breathing down my neck,
I thought I might be sick!
The Head he shouted loudly,
I felt my face turn red.
I said that I was sorry,
He sadly shook his head.
I crept out the office,
My worried friends were there.
I skipped gaily to the playground.
As if I didn't care.

Kim Blundell (10)
Bablake Junior School
Coventry, Notts

What Do Girls Do at Play Time?

What do girls do at play time?
Cuddle up in corners and ...
Tell secrets with each other.
Play hopscotch with friends
And do the s...p...l...i...t...s!
And boys go Hoo Hoo
And the girls say ...
Stop!

What do boys do at play time?
Play football and play 'it'!
And play Penalties
And say Hoo Hoo to the girls
And the girls say ...
Stop!

Kelly Haylett (7)
Townhill Junior School
Southampton, Hampshire
(Age Category Winner)

Sound and Noise

I'm walking down the yard
People playing Pogs and football
Pogs clink, footballs thump.
Shouts of high voices
Can't hear the birds
Wind swishes like water
Past my ears
I can see the trees move
But I can't hear them.
At the end of break
A whistle goes, and the bell
Screaming and ringing.
Then it is quiet
You can hear the birds and the wind.

James Wright (11)
Holywell Middle School
Cranfield, Bedfordshire

The History Room

This is how we were taught,
These four walls were our inspiration.
A chink of sunshine through the curtains
Throws light onto fading essays and wall displays
Heaped unlovingly,
  cast away on the floor.
The old musty smell of text books
Draws me to the corner,
  a heap of pages,
    broken spines.
Have they no respect for the way we learnt?
These computer kids,
  robotically minded
Prototype people,
  genetically changed.
I see dust floating in a channel of light.
Floating relics of history,
    ashes of a different time.

Katherine Rogers (16)
Romsey, Hampshire

Grandma's Late Again

Grandma never went straight to school,
She played with her friends
And fell in the mud
Picked all the redcurrants
A red berry bud.
Grandma never went straight to school,
She danced in the lanes
And jumped over stiles
She climbed apple trees
And ran for miles.
Grandma never went straight to school,
And when it was time to go
She ran there hair flying back
With clothes so tattered and torn
They resembled an old grubby sack,
Grandma never went straight to school,
When the teachers told Nan
That Grandma was late
Nan shrugged and sighed
And bore the weight
   that,
Grandma *never* went straight to school.

Natalie Branston (15)
Gillingham, Dorset

I Bet You'll Enjoy It

The Magic Shop

In my shop you can buy
a beautiful rainbow straight from the sky
the sound of cry from a horse's neigh,
and a can of sunshine for a wintery day.
A jar of longlife news
and a bottle full of views
a packet of tear drops for an unhappy face
and a box of glittered candies for a very sour place.
A beautiful bucket of sparkling dew
the scent from a rose especially for you
a gleaming shell from the sea
and a black and yellow buzzing bee.
A marvellous box of fantasy wishes
and tiny scales from tiny fishes
a shining fountain full of sand
the sound from a vibrant orchestra band.
Shelves of magic everywhere
magic here magic there.
In my shop you can buy
a beautiful rainbow straight from the sky.

Simone Milani (9)
Malorees Junior School
London

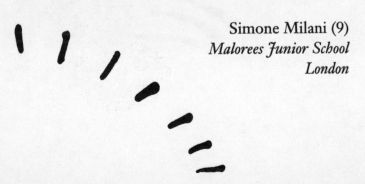

My Violin

Delicate instrument, an elegant shape,
Its dusty strings covered with a deep resin,
Its orange body tinted with bronze mist,
The black keys at my hand,
All smooth and dipped,
And the spiral staircase at the top
Waiting right before me.

Katherine Byard (10)
Our Lady of Pity School
Wirral, Merseyside

Snape Maltings

The warm curve of music
Floated gently like a rainbow
Of oil on water.
Then, as I stared
At the conductor,
Carefully counting
The beats in my head,
It changed to an inexorable
Swirling mass
Of merging colours.
An invisible silver thread
Glimmered and intensified
Between me and the
Monochrome conductor.
The audience – pale dabs
On shadow – seemed to dim,
And the orchestra aged
To a sepia photograph.
The black and white choir
Squeezed in around the edge
Of my vision.
A moment's age of silence throbbed
When the music died away.
Only its memory
Hung in the air.
The silver thread tightened,
Glistening,
As I stared steadily

At the bright red carnation
In the conductor's lapel.
The excited silence
Buzzed in my head.
I dared myself to look away.
Once, twice the thread held firm.
Then sheets of music rustled to my right;
I glanced across and applause broke
Like a sudden-crumpled wrapper.
I looked up;
The conductor was bowing.
The thread had been broken.
I closed my score
And tried not to mind that
The sparkling silver had been
Brushed so quickly away.

Sarah Hunter (15)
Stowmarket, Suffolk

March

I pick up my pencil,
Striped red and black.
It stands to attention in my hand.
I open my book,
Flick through the thin white leaves.
Like the bark on a tree, they are already covered
With lines and whorls,
Silent music.

But then I come upon an empty page,
A leaf with no life.
Only a few faint lines
Like the asymmetrical bars in a gym –
But my mind is blank,
There are no supple bodies clothed in brightly-coloured
    leotards.
Tentatively, I draw a graceful treble clef
And I can feel
The fibres of the paper
Pulling a thin grey ribbon of lead
Through my pencil.

Next comes the time signature:
Four beats in a bar
For I plan to write a march.
Suddenly, ominous as distant thunder,
A drum role reverberates within my head,
A trumpet blasts, splitting the air;
A march is forming, muffled still,

Magnificent and measured.

As the notes come pouring through my ears,
Tramping into my brain,
I see the soldiers advancing,
A thin brave line of scarlet rolling forward
With their tall hats and gleaming ebony boots
And their brass buttons.

The clarinets wail like a spoilt child;
Fanfare of trombones, a clash of cymbals
Heralding the melody, haunting and stately.
Padded stick and poised palm held ready,
Brass and woodwind unfurled like banners,
A controlled and pervading splendour.

It is a victory march.
I see it now.
Why else would the music ring out with such exultancy?
Triumphant pomp and circumstance.
The last loud joyful note is played
And as the echo dies away
I open my eyes, look down at my book.
An almost empty page stares back at me;
One treble clef, one time signature in 44 time.

Yet resounding still in my memory
The march plays on.

Nancy Groves (12)
Wimbledon High School
Wimbledon, London
(Poet of the Year)

Hands

Hands can pick things up like pencils
Hands can be kind and helpful
Hands wave at people you know
Hands clap when you listen to music
Hands help you eat and drink when it's tea time
Hands can push people when they be unkind
Hands are so helpful when you use them
Hands are beautiful.

Tamsyn Sear (7)
Crossways Junior School
Thornbury, Bristol

The Artist

I sat there
Uncertain of what might develop
Perched on a stool
Inside a half-empty room

He entered so gracefully
Gliding like a swan
He dived into my soul
And studied me intensely

He began to work
At which he was fluent
The task, soon finished
My approval desired

I feasted my eyes upon the exhibit
I was anxious to see, but
To my surprise I did not witness my portrait
Instead, a young girl looked back at me

She was crouched in the corner
Of a massive, bare room
He had not studied my outer form
Instead, my inner emotions

Sarah Norcup (15)
Clough Hall School
Stoke-on-Trent, Staffs

Second Class

You are desecrated,
dirtied by strange,
curving lines of blue, maybe
black, and often
others.

Bent over, you are
ignominiously thrust into
a confining, dark space.

You are, at present,
experiencing claustrophobia.

There is a slurping,
wet sound, and
then you're immured.

You are taken
to a small brick
building, and your
death certificate is carefully pasted
onto the
top right-hand corner
of your prison.

Then, you are carelessly
pushed into the

gaping,
dark maw
of the postbox.

Thomas Yates (14)
Maharishi School
Ormskirk, Lancashire
(Roald Dahl Wondercrump School Award)

The Chapter That Got Away

I am the chapter that got away.
The part of the book you wanted to read,
but couldn't discover
between these covers.
I am the vital page that got torn out by the
previous reader's nephew.
The middle of the story
that tells how it happened.
I am the source of the intention.
I am the motive of the killer.
I am the riddle that remains a riddle,
for I am the chapter that got away.

Fehim Uddin (14)
Pimlico School
Pimlico, London

Railway Station

The train sounds like my mum's old banger
But much louder.
I hear the bags of coal
Being thrown into the steam train.
It sounds like a big rock
Being thrown against a wall.

The lady shouts.
PEEP.
'Get out the way.
The train is leaving platform number 29.
Thank you.'
PEEP PEEP!

She sounds like my mum
Telling my brother off.

People shout with excitement.
They sound like lions roaring.

The railway track is long and thin.
It can electrocute you.
Make your hair stand on end.

The real train was like my brother's toy one
But not as noisy.
The train was trembling along the track.
Trying to stay on the track.

I grabbed onto the green rail,
I climbed up the seven, slippery steps.

Off we went into the beautiful country.

Samantha Bayley (7)
Hilperton CE Primary School
Trowbridge, Wilts.

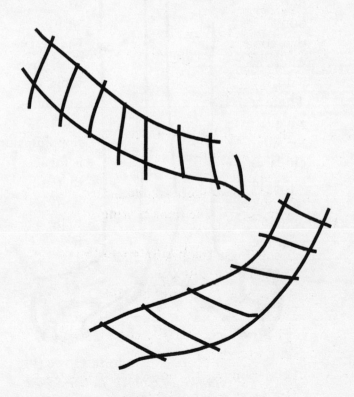

The short summery Thin Thong song

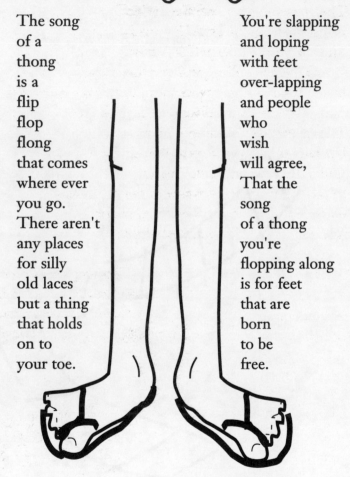

The song
of a
thong
is a
flip
flop
flong
that comes
where ever
you go.
There aren't
any places
for silly
old laces
but a thing
that holds
on to
your toe.

You're slapping
and loping
with feet
over-lapping
and people
who
wish
will agree,
That the
song
of a thong
you're
flopping along
is for feet
that are
born
to be
free.

John Howe (9)
Hawkesley Church Junior School
Hawkesley, Birmingham

Second Home

Ending the hours of road, sea, road again,
Yawn smothers smile as the car crackles on.
The criss and cross of the brittle fence
Is lost in the grass and the unruly ferns,
And the wisteria drips blue syrup
Down the crumbling white of the house's hide.
Inside bakes, schnapps with candles, cakes with dust,
And cobweb-covered in the cellar's shade
The quiet smell of safety lingers.
Upstairs unwraps the parcel on the bed
And dolls awaiting rediscovery
In boxes stuffed with more forgotten things.
Outside, the trees are freshly echoing,
And I'm pretending on the swings.

Timothy Watts (16)
The Holy Trinity School
Crawley, West Sussex
(Age Category Winner)

Letter from a Rocking Horse

I'm squashed in the attic
Tucked right in the corner.
Nobody's seen me for a hundred years.
Hidden in this gloomy prison,
How I want to cry.
When I was young children adored me
Played with me all the time
Fighting to climb upon my back.
Henry played cowboys and indians.
And Ann sat her dolls on my saddle
Taking them for a ride.
Life was lovely
And I was attractive,
With a pretty horse-hair mane
and tail.
My back dappled grey.
But now I'm a disgrace.
An eye is missing
My back is yellowed with age
And the paint's peeling off.
The hairs in my mane and tail
Have been plucked out
And my mouth's set in a faded smile.
So if you can make my smile brighter
Come and find me

Ride me and make me happy.
Love, Rose, a Victorian rocking horse.

Aimee Cottam (7)
Lowes Wong Junior School
Southwell, Nottinghamshire

My Dolly Molly

I've got a dolly and her name is Molly.
She is very very jolly,
And she loves sweet lollies.
Her friend is Polly.
And she says OH GOLLY!

My friend's got a dolly and her name is Polly
And she is not very jolly.
She hates sweet lollies.
Her friend is Molly
And she never says GOLLY!

Penelope Jones (4)
Weymouth, Dorset

Ice Skating

I stared at the silver blades,
Sharp enough to slice stone.
Slowly, I tied the lace
And gazed at the boots,
Then at the ice.
I got up,
Wobbled and flapped around,
Like a fledgling learning to fly,
About to make that final leap
Which would decide his future ...
Fall or fly?
I stepped onto the ice.
I seemed to be suspended by a thin thread.
I stood on ice!
I took my first step.
BANG!
I felt the coldness through my gloves.
A tiny drop of blood dripped
Onto the chipped ice
Where I'd skidded over.
It stained the ice a deep red,
Redness which seeped through,
Like rain flooding raked soil.
Tears filled my eyes.
I grabbed the railings
And heaved myself up.
My feet didn't follow me.

They attracted each other:
Like two magnets, they touched at opposite ends.
I was still like that fledgling.
I pulled myself along the railings,
Like a spider climbing its thread.
My feet moved around the ice,
In every direction,
But not forward.
It was time to let go.
I pushed myself away from the side.
I seemed to fly.
I could skate!

Elizabeth Stanyer (13)
Halesworth Middle School
Halesworth, Suffolk

Jeopardy

'I bet you'll enjoy it,
I know that you will.'
The ski man assured,
As I paid at the till.
I didn't believe him,
But nodded and smiled.
'Five forty,' he grinned,
'Half price for a child.'
As I entered the ski slopes,
I shuddered in fright.
The slopes were so steep,
And just look at the height!
As I built up my courage,
Tried not to look ill,
I felt a huge push,
And I slid down the hill ...
The people below me,
(Advanced Skiing Team)
Looked like Lego figures,
Except, they could SCREAM!
The wind slashed my cheeks,
And swiped at my hair.
I looked up to heaven,
And whispered a prayer.
The trees rushed towards me,
Their arms stretched right out.
They waved me along

To my death bed, (no doubt!).
I furrowed my eyebrows,
And tried to look calm,
But it's just not too easy,
When heading for harm.
I squeezed up my eyes,
As I swung round a bend.
Then I tripped, and I fell,
And that was the end ...
OK! I admit it,
It wasn't that bad!
It was only a bump on the knee
That I had.
So, I climbed up the mountain,
To the ski lift I clung.
Caught sight of the ski man,
And stuck out my tongue!

Danielle Meinrath (10)
Channing School
Highgate, London

Spoon

i am,
despite my diffidence,
as the bruise i leave in the milk of your cereal
clears,
graceful,
slender,
in my own way
musical.

Rose Beauchamp (16)
King Edward VI School for Girls
Edgbaston, Birmingham

Giant

Big as a dinosaur,
Gentle as a flower,
Hopping like the sea crashing down,
A giant running through the sand,
Scrunching the stones,
Crying, making a swimming pool with his tears.

Monica Campbell-Scott (6)
Handford Hall CP
Ipswich, Suffolk

Oh No

Oh I hate it when I go for …
Football practice!
When I have the ball they all
Push me over.
He gives me a yellow card
When I didn't do
Anything
And when I score a goal they always
Kick me in the leg.

Bradley Watts (7)
Townhill Junior School
Southampton, Hampshire

When I Went to Wembley

I went to Wembley with my friend
to see Liverpool against Southend.
We wanted seats behind the goal
But found ourselves by the corner-flag pole.
The teams came out in red and green
And everyone stood to sing *God Save the Queen*.

Liverpool started brightly with a strong attack.
But Southend wouldn't be beaten and quickly came back.
The action flowed end to end
With both teams needing to defend.
But after 40 minutes Liverpool scored
How their supporters roared and roared.

And till the end it stayed like that
And at the end I bought a Liverpool hat.
Then we went back home
and did this poem.

Matthew Evans (7)
St Luke's Junior School
Brighton, East Sussex

Fan to Goalkeeper

There you were, standing tall,
You were solid,
Solid as the three posts on your sides,
Infallible ...
Until the ball struck,
It flew slow and curving
Round the cowering wall,
I saw my admiration crumble
As you leapt,
It was not enough.
The net shuddered,
Forty thousand roared,
I cried.

Roddie Gibb (16)
Hutchesons' Grammar School
Glasgow

Rugby Match Recipe

Locate a pitch with posts at either end,
Prepare an egg-shaped ball.
Fry six gormless hooligans who are referred to as props.
Boil tempers to the extreme for half an hour,
Then add three teaspoonfuls of riot,
Allow the riot to simmer for a further hour.
Cool gently and resume play,
Slice the element of sportsmanship into infinitesimally
small pieces.
Whisk the pitch into a brown mass sprinkled with stud
    marks
and the occasional pool of blood.
Add a pinch of clever play,
Which frustrates the brainless hooligans further!
Toss the ball to the backs and watch them sauté through
    the defence.
Prepare try in cooking oil and top up with wine.
The whistle is blown, the game ends,
And here is a rugby match of the finest ingredients
Perfectly prepared, *bon appetit*!

Jonny White (10)
Mowden School
Hove, East Sussex
(School of the Year)

I am an Isolation Hospital

Friendship

Hard to break up,
Unless you dig deep at the roots,
Like ivy, climbing skywards nonstop,
Until separated by success or destiny.
Beautiful as Venus in space,
It's like a clown-fish and coral,
Hot and cold as a sunspot,
Hard as as a conker,
Soft as air,
Firm as a building,
Blinding as a lamp,
Fading through time;
But never forgotten.

Timothy Eldridge (11)
Downsend School
Leatherhead, Surrey

Divided

There's something strange when I enter the room
I can sense a kind of emptiness,
Some sort of tension in the air.
I feel uncomfortable when I sit with you both
Wanting to speak words to you
But there's something stopping them coming out of my
    mouth.
I leave you quietly behind me and then I hear it
The noise of anger breaking out to the surface
Rage and hatred being expressed between each other.
I sit alone and cry as the two of you grow further apart.
The love that was once there has disappeared
And now when I see you it's as if it never existed at all.
In the end one of you left and you left me behind with the
    other,
Picking up the pieces of what was broken
Trying to fill the empty space hovering around us.
When I look back I remember the happiness we all shared
But as the days go by it gets harder and harder
And all I see is torment and friction.
So once when I wanted us all to be together
To share everything like we used to
I now think to myself it's better as it is.

Nicola Robinson (17)
Shena Simon College
Manchester

Echoes in the Hall

'She's not feeling well.'
States the voice
As flat and cold as the
Bare floors.
'... feeling well?'
Mocks the voice
As quiet and gentle as the
Morning breeze.

'I don't want to see you again!'
Cries the voice
As angry and cruel as the
Mid-winter snows,
'... see you again?'
Taunts the voice
As soft and warm as the
Old blanket.

'She doesn't want to go out.'
Insists the voice
As forceful and persuasive as the
Rusty crowbar.
' ... want to go out?'
Invites the voice
As bright and hopeful as the
New day.
'Goodbye?'

Asks the voice
As unsure and afraid as the
New-born foal
'Goodbye.'
Echoes the voice
As final and firm as the
Thud of the door.

Sonya Cotton (16)
Coleraine High School
Coleraine, Co, Londonderry

When Nobody Wants to Play

When nobody
wants to play
with me,
I feel like
an old book,
put away in the attic
and
forgotten about.

Anna Radmore (8)
Darell School
Richmond, Surrey

HIV Positive

Just like a couple, you and I, but
not the same.

In school they judged you to be clever –
I found you kind.

In time I saw that you were like me:
we shared
minds

But there were always differences between us.

For a time I did not notice them,
Save for when unwitting comments earned
Our soft disdain, the liberal eyebrow raised:
Irony, your secret made us stronger.

But time ...

(the verbal shrug)

... time wastes away.

One of our many last evenings together:
our yellow beach where waves do secret damage
to the smooth face of the sand:
here where time is not defined

by sunrise or by sunsets
but by your passing
consciousness

Is it true that you are dying?

the dark approaches and
we talk rapidly:

death has no hold
on great men's work

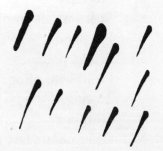

I plead

Then silence.

I watch you
watch the sea birds breed

Catherine McAleese (15)
Ripon Grammar School
Ripon, North Yorkshire
(Age Category Winner)

Phone

Sit by phone,
Watch phone,
Stare into phone,
Drum fingers on phone,
Whistle,
Nothing.
Speak nicely to phone,
Pat phone,
Stroke phone,
Plead with phone,
To ring.
Nothing.
Offer phone last Rolo,
Phone rings.
Jump.
Pout lips,
Cross legs,
Toss hair,
Pick up phone.
'Hello, Mum, I'm fine!'
Slam down phone.
Wait,
And wait.
Nothing.
Hit phone,
Swear at phone,
Does he own a phone?
Yes.

Does he have my number?
Yes.
Lift receiver,
Dial number,
Engaged.
What if he's talking to somebody else?
What if it's HER?
It is.
He hates me.
I hate him.
Phone rings –
Disconnect phone.

Rebecca Youens (13)
Dr Challoner's High School
Little Chalfont, Buckinghamshire
(Age Category Winner)

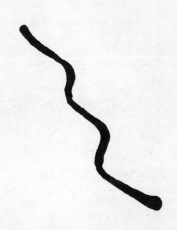

Listening to Bruch

He stands.
The sunlight on his hair.
The golden glow
Frames his face.
I watch him
As he puts his bow
To the strings.
I hear
  faint
    disjointed
      chords ...
... his tuning up.

And then
The melody
The adagio from Bruch's violin concerto.

The closed door
Distorts the sound.
Yet still
Bruch
Hits a nerve
As an arpeggio bursts inside me.

But now
My view is lost.
She stands
In my way.
I no longer see

His face
 his eyes
  his lips
   his hair ...
But still the Bruch
Fills my head.

Cassie Barber (17)
Stourport High School
Stourport-on-Severn, Worcestershire

The Twilight

You left before the twilight,
And I just wanted to tell you,
That the twilight was beautiful:
The sky a myriad of mysterious dark shades;
Tufts of snowy white and deep blue,
Racing to blot out the first stars,
Across the purple breathless sky.
And the shivering moon with its pale halo,
Reflected on the sea.

You should have stayed for the twilight,
If not for me.

Fabiola Smolowik (15)
Forest (Girls') School
Snaresbrook, London
(Age Category Winner)

Of Narcissus and Reflections

What were his reflections?
That beautiful Greek youth,
As he knelt on the warm earth beside that quiet pool,
So many thousands of years ago.

Did he remember the anguished lovers he had spurned,
indifferent to their pain?
His hair fell thick and gleaming, golden as a cornfield.
Did he consider the unhappiness and the longing he had left
behind him?
Dappled light played on his smooth olive skin, fingering
the nape of his neck.
Did he notice in the heat of the afternoon, the wood nymph's
desolate cry?
He was flawless and solitary, a lovely autistic, untouched
and untouchable.
Did he think of the mortals and immortals who had craved his
embrace?
His face was perfection; the arch of his eyebrow, the curve
of his lips.
Did he regret those days and nights spent alone, obsessively
waiting?
And his eyes gazed, large and blank and blue like sapphires,
As he leant forward to drink.

What were his reflections?
That beautiful Greek youth,
As he knelt in a haze of love and despair beside that quiet
    pool,
So many thousands of years ago.

Nancy Groves (12)
Wimbledon High School
Wimbledon, London
(Poet of the Year)

Jealousy

Jealousy is like a great black
hole sucking everything
in.
Jealousy is like a fungus
growing and growing inside.
Like a monster punching me inside.
Like a star burning up.
Like a bee sting right inside
that's
what
jealousy is

Terry Baylis (8)
Binfield C of E Primary School
Bracknell, Berkshire
(Age Category Winner)

Windows

Seven weeks have now gone by,
Still at night he haunts me.
Breathing coldly upon my neck
And whispering ever so slowly.
Open windows make for chilly nights,
All tucked up in your bed.
But open minds make room for him,
Running riot in my head.

Moving, running, silently fighting,
I long to be free once more.
Old love will never leave my side
Of this I can be sure.
He dances in my nightmares,
Sings songs to fill my dreams.
With his knife he cuts my heart
Crying as it gleams.
Open windows make for cold nights,
All tucked up in your bed.

But open hearts make for misery
With this butcher in my head.

Hayley Johnson (17)
Astley Cooper School
Hemel Hempstead, Hertfordshire

Lament of a Pear

The pear stands there
On the table
Gazing at the apple
Whose delicate rosy blush
Shines seductively

'You are the queen,' he thinks.
'Perched upon the shoulders
Of your fellows, in your woven throne.
Where I am but as unworthy as
A banana, to be before your grace.

Look down at my rags,
Brown and green with grime.
How can I compare with your
Soft red dress and teal lapels?
So I stand here, below your worship,

And admire.'

Matalin Hatchard (13)
Maharishi School
Ormskirk, Lancashire
(Roald Dahl Wondercrump School Award)

Discard

Old lover, dead meat
He has stolen my friends,
I am an isolation hospital.
Even the girl with the speech defect
will not sit by me.
They say it is official.
I swear I am only a visitor here ...

They shake their heads,
I imagine they are fruit machines
spilling coins along with sound words,
or scared old men
rocking in the corners of children's books,
or hiding in the cupboards of the
girl with the greying socks who
let them roll down and then folded them
like secrets into her shoes.

They turn and stare,
Faces like moons, but chins
like cruel paintings done by
the boys who say they love you.
Teasing they mock your features,
Competing to be the first to see
your blank raw eyes.
Your pupils disturb like crazed moths.

They are invisible as if someone
had stolen them for sweets,
and paid you with the tiny bodies
of dead mince.

Francesca Platt (17)
Canon Slade School
Bolton, Lancashire
(Age Category Winner)

Fruits of ...

I always thought passion fruit
would be bigger,
They look rather like dark
golf balls,
Maybe even more wrinkly,
I always thought they'd be bigger,
rounder and more full.
I think it's the name,
It just gives the impression
that there would be more.

Susan Robertson (17)
Loxton, Avon

Second Thoughts

I collapse into my chair and start
Knocking on my door
I get up to answer but feel
Hi!
She walks in and accuses me of
Having friends for dinner
I knock her to the floor and she knows that it's
Possible to borrow a knife
As the knife slits her throat she screams with
Pleasure as I hand her the utensil
I plunge it deep into her
Heartfelt thanks for lending it to her
I feel no regret. Not at all
Sorry for bothering me
As the earth covers her body, I can hear her
Knocking on my front door
Never again do I have to worry about her
Returning my knife
She will never
See me tomorrow

Lizzie Elliott (16)
Aberdeen, Scotland

My Heart is a Sea Monster

Consciousness

Consciousness expresses itself through creation,
This world we live in is the dream of the creator,
Dreamers come and go in the twinkling of an eye but the dream
lives on.
On many an occasion, when I am dreaming, I have felt touched
by something sacred,
In those moments, I felt my spirit soar, and become one with
everything that exists.
I become the stars and the moon,
I become the lover and the beloved,
I become the victor and the vanquished,
I become the master and the slave,
I become the singer and the song,
I become the knower and the known,
I keep on dreaming then it is the eternal dream of creation,
The creator and the creation merge into one wholeness of joy,
I keep on dreaming ... and dreaming ... and dreaming,
until there
is only ...
The dream.

Craig Abbott (14)
Thorne Grammar School
Doncaster, South Yorkshire

Space Is

Space is a peculiar thing,
It is something containing everything,
And everything containing nothing.
Space to me is a blank piece of paper
Waiting to be filled.
Space in mind where thoughts should be.
Finger space,
Space between words.
And space to breathe and think.
Inner space,
Outer space,
Your space,
My space:
Space to face the emptiness of a blank page.

Ella Worth (10)
Gosforth Central Middle School
Gosforth, Tyne and Wear

Sea Monster Poem

My heart is a sea monster floating in the sea
My hair is all green, my toes are all blue
If you can see a sea monster
You can see me too.

I'm all sad and lonely, I haven't any friends
I'm drifting in the ocean all by myself
I'm a sea monster, I have nobody else.
Can you see my beauty? I need someone to help.

My heart is a sea monster floating in the sea
If you can see beauty – you can see me.

Alexandra Freckleton (5)
Abingdon, Northamptonshire

Drowning

Swimming in circles
Talking to the vanished floor
Come up and touch me.

Lisa Shovelar (9)
Townhill Junior School
Southampton, Hampshire
(Age Category Winner)

If Only

I'm a
discontented cordless Kenwood kettle.

I dream
of greasy crumbs and
four-slice bread slots.
A toaster!
A shiny
green
Morphy Richards toaster, with
Variable Browning Control.

And I'd slouch
with my Frozen Bread Setting
and my Touch-sensitive Reheat Button,
while popping reassuringly ...

I didn't have the intellect.

Luke Yates (11)
Maharishi School
Ormskirk, Lancashire
(Age Category Winner)
(Roald Dahl Wondercrump School Award)

The Big Chance

It came along at a million miles per hour,
A train,
Speeding past those who weren't talented enough,
Didn't want it badly enough,
And stopped at me.

The doors opened wide,
I had my ticket in my hand,
But I stopped to think.
I took a seat in the cold station,
And thought.

Weighed up the pros and the cons,
Then decided it was what I wanted.
I ran to the platform,
Ticket in hand,
It had gone!

The lady at the ticket box explained,
They saw someone else,
Someone who had climbed aboard,
Without thinking.

I tried to run after it.
I ran as fast as I could,
But it had gone,
Off into the sunset,

Leaving me stranded,
In the middle of nowhere,
With a void ticket,
And a faceful of smoke.

I went back to the station, in tears.
The lady at the ticket box just smiled,
She had seen it all before.

Jenny Jolly (14)
St Leonard's RC Comprehensive
Durham, County Durham

Lost Hope

I grab at stars,
Sweeping my hand across the heavens,
Hanging on to sharp chunks of hope that
    cut my palm.
Carefully, eagerly I prize open my fingers
And find I have captured only slivers of darkness.

Eve-Louise Walker (14)
Tewkesbury, Gloucestershire

Disappointment

Disappointment is like a disease.
It will eat you up inside
And spit you out
Into a gutter of sadness
That will hold you prisoner
Until you fight it with hope ...
    and escape.

Peter Cummings (10)
Parsons Down Junior School
Thatcham, Berkshire

Loneliness

Loneliness is a chimney on a dark winter night,
Or the ancient ruin of a distant and desolate church.
A single bird searching vainly for a mate,
Or a solitary island lost in the sea.
Loneliness is a whale searching for the pack,
Or a little child alone in a forest.
A cave with no visitors,
Or a book left on the shelf, never read.

Peter Alpass (11)
Downsend School
Leatherhead, Surrey

LINES FROM INSIDE A LION

The Wuzzy Wasps

The wuzzy wasps of Wasperton
Are buzzing round the pears
Eating all the ripe ones
They think the orchard's theirs.

Kevin Hunter (7)
Gerrards Cross School
Gerrards Cross, Buckinghamshire

I Am a Woodlouse

I am a woodlouse
I do you no harm
I am a woodlouse
  and I am very small
But when you come to
  pick me up,
I turn into a ball.

Stephanie Nightingale (6)
Combs Ford CP School
Stowmarket, Suffolk

Jasmin

I have a black puppy
Jasmin's her name.
She's five-months-old
and thinks everything a game.
She chews Daddy's flowers.
She digs great big holes,
The garden looks like
We've got lots of moles.
When she sees her lead
She bounds up and down
She gets so excited
I can't calm her down.
She has Weetabix for breakfast
and Pal for her tea
And when she has finished
She sleeps on my knee.
I tickle her tummy.
I stroke her back.
We lie there together
And both have a nap.

Katie Bird (7)
Westhouses Primary School
Westhouses, Derbyshire

What Does Toby Need . . ?

It's taken some time,
But he's soon here to stay,
Toby's happy and healthy,
I like him that way.

And so I've been thinking,
Of things he may need,
And just to remind me,
I'll start with the lead.

Some bowls and a collar,
A disc with a name,
Some toys he can play with,
Again and again.

He'll need some brushing and combing,
Sometimes a bath,
To get all the dirt off,
I don't think he'll laugh.

He'll need some good training,
To sit and to stay,
He'll be so obedient,
He won't run away.

It's time for injections,
A trip to the vets,
We might have to drag him,
Don't worry Toby not yet!

And so I remember,
To complete my list,
I've thought of most items,
But something I've missed.

In all of this thinking,
One thing I must do,
Is to hug and to stroke you,
And say 'I LOVE YOU'.

Anna Coulton (11)
(1981 – 1994)

The Fastest Chaser Of All

When I was small and had to stay indoors
I would chase my family to prove I was fast.
I would hide in dark shadows close to the floor
And pounce on their legs as they walked past.
When I was bigger and my family too slow
I chased other things, my favourite a ball.
I'd bounce it so hard I'd not see where it would go
Under the sofa, behind the plant in the hall,
But always I'd catch it, always I'd know
The way it would bounce as it came off the wall.
Everyone said it just went to show
That I was the fastest chaser of all.
Then when we moved to a house on a hill
With walls of white and a red roof of tiles,
The wind blew so hard nothing ever was still,
But again I was the fastest chaser for miles.
I'd chase the leaves and the insects until
It was time to go home, my face one big smile,
And dream in the night of the speed and the thrill
Of chasing fast things all of the while.
And then a new challenge, too fast for words,
Flew round the cottage on the swiftest of wings.
I discovered the thrill of chasing the birds,
As they ate in our garden of peanuts and things.
But then one day, as I tried to hide,
I got the biggest shock of them all.
With a tail like a rainbow and wings so wide
Arrived a bird that looked twelve feet tall!

I jumped from the bush and raced inside
And shouted 'Dad, I've had a really big shock!
What's that bird?' Dad glanced outside
And laughed 'It's just Charles the Peacock.'
He picked me up and stroked my face.
'Don't worry, you won't get bitten.
He's very gentle but too big to chase,
You funny little kitten.'

Drew Bridger (8)
Embley Park Junior School,
Romsey, Hants

I Don't Know Why

I don't know why
my cat runs away from me
I don't know why
my cat likes soggy stuff
I don't know why
she sicks on the floor
I don't know why

Tristan Welsted-Robins (5)
Barnsbury Infant School
Woking, Surrey

Piglet

The cardboard box tremored,
With nervous vibrations,
The blanket was a mountain,
Which he could not climb.
His umbilical cord hung down,
Like a grey worm.
He stuck his snout in the corner of cardboard,
Searching for his mother.
He was four hours old
And lucky to be alive.
As they tried feeding him through a rubber glove fake
    udder
He squeaked as if someone had trodden on a toy dog bone
And milk squirted sideways drenching his body hairs,
Dripping like dabs of watery white paint
On his shining body, not used to the lights.
As his mouth opened,
High pitched snuffles bellowed out.
The scratches on his back looked like open veins.
They were from fighting his brothers and sisters,
In a scrabble for their mother's milk.
The over-sized cloth ears
Hid his squirming eyes.
Bits of dry grass stuck to his shivering body,
The tail sticking out like a ringlet of permed hair.
Calmly, I stroked his pinkish-white body.
And as I ran my fingers up and down his back,
Small dimpled ripples subsided.

Then, as she picked him up,
He scrumpled up his keyhole snout.
And made such a piercing noise for such a tiny creature.
He was back to his rightful owner.

Tessa Hart (12)
Halesworth Middle School
Halesworth, Suffolk
(Age Category Winner)

Pig World and Human World

They've got oinks,
We've got words,
We've got friends,
They've got herds.

They've got pens,
We've got houses,
They've got mates,
We've got spouses.

We've got clothes,
They're all nude,
They've got slop,
We've got food.

Their lives are quick
Our lives are slow.
They've got no time,
But they don't know.

Zoe Harrigan (12)
Cator Park School
Beckenham, Kent

The shack

In the beaten shack
At the bottom of our allotment
Lie old mattress springs,
Covered in fine cobwebs
Which are spun into Aboriginal patterns of wisdom.
In the centre of each cobweb,
Hangs a creamy spider skeleton,
Crispy and dried with age.
In the corner of the shack,
Damp grass and moss
Grow through a peeping crack.
A big fat toad lives there.
He's a murky green
And the knobbles on his back
Look like an old lady's bony knuckles.
The old horse named Douglas
Grazes by the weather-worn shack.
His mane tangles, wiry,
In a clawing branch.
His hot breath is steam,
A billowing cloud which trails after a train.
In the beaten shack,
At the bottom of our allotment,
Unknown ancient treasures lie deep.

Naomi Everett (13)
Halesworth Middle School
Halesworth, Suffolk

The Horse

Standing lonely,
Like a bullied child.
Tied up in the corner,
He longs for the wild.

The soft black eyes,
Of his gentle face,
Seem warm and comforting,
In this cold dark place.

His muscles tense up,
As he takes the strain.
With a challenging rear,
He tears away from the chain.

Out into the night,
And away like a bird.
He gallops and gallops,
Until no more he is heard.

He looks like a picture,
As he flies over the ground,
With his neck outstretched,
Not making a sound.

A piercing whinny
Cuts through the night sky.
He stops dead in his tracks,
His head held up high.

Far in the distance
They come into sight,
Three galloping horses,
Two black and one white.

The horse, he stands watching,
This magnificent three.
Then as a foursome together,
They run to be free.

Laura Allen (15)
Thomas Alleyne's High School
Uttoxeter, Staffordshire

Fox

Then I saw him,
The colour of autumn gold,
Small and light footed,
Padding through a sea of leaves.
Beyond him was a setting sun,
Amber in the evening sky.
Time had stopped,
The wind was still,
And the fox was passing by.

Elyse Doran (12)
Port Regis School
Shaftesbury, Dorset

The Hunt

The hounds of the hunt are ready to
bite on a cold and frosty night.
A fox is spotted,
They chase it but . . .
it disappears in the darkness.
A hare is running through the grass.
They chase it but . . .
it is much too fast.
A deer is in sight,
They shoot at it but . . .
miss!
It runs off and hope is lost for the hunt.

Edward Badham (7)
Neston CP School
Neston, Wiltshire

Death

He lay dying
His red hair matted
And streaked with blood.
His eyes, once a golden brown,
Were going dull.
His legs were stiffening in death,
His breathing became laboured,
He tried to move, to struggle,

But it was no use.
He lay there by the roadside,
No one came to bury him
Because no one cared about him.
After all, he was just a fox.

Debbie Skelly (15)
Hunterhouse College
Finaghy, Belfast

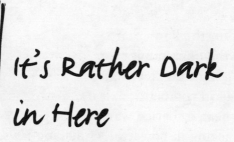

It's Rather Dark in Here

I am writing these lines from
inside a lion
And it's rather dark in here!
So excuse the writing that
may not be too clear.
But I am afraid to tell you
last night I got too near.

Oliver Oldman (7)
Gerrards Cross School
Gerrards Cross, Buckinghamshire

Hyenas

An injured springbok
Is enclosed in a ring of hungry hyenas.
Wicked laugh, dirty, rotting teeth,
Spotted coat, demented torturers,
Slinking towards the cowering creature.
A terrible pause before the hunters close in for the kill.

Terrified squealing – the injured animal is torn apart –
Its last breath rattles from its throat
And dark death brings relief from agony.

Fighting for the lion's share
Without the lion's nobility –
Snatching, fighting, tearing,
Devouring in competition,
Tearing meat, a snarled warning,
Bones cracking in powerful, crunching jaws,
Blood-red muscles ripping apart.

Stomachs filled,
The hyenas pack together –
A happy family.
Young ones play in the sinking sun,
Leaping, rolling, chasing,
Cubs nestle in for warmth and safety of a mother's fur,
Grandfather is stretched out,
Relaxed,
Satisfied.

Henry Tyler (12)
Dartford, Kent

Cheetah

The dust rises like hot mist
Over the sun-baked plains;
Pale yellow and stale, dead
As the plant life all around.

Like an athlete poised
Ready to sprint, Cheetah,
The Linford Christie of
The animal world.

Its gold medal, a deer,
Grazes innocently;
Unaware of danger
From the king of sprinters.

The starting gun explodes.
The Cheetah bursts its blocks.
Rivals are all beaten,
First prize is never shared.

The dust settles . . .

Rebekah Crowther (14)
Stourport High School
Stourport-on-Severn, Worcestershire

Old Man of Africa

Old man's face with wrinkled ears,
Tusks that grew for years and years.
Swaying trunk, sharp, dark eyes,
Tail that flicked away the flies.

Thump and Rumble, through the Jungle
Elephant slowly plods his way
Squashing grass, twigs, plants and flowers,
African Elephant, poacher's prey.

The Gun is fired, the birds take off
The Great Beast stops and looks around;
Sees the poachers stalking forward,
Taking aim to strike him down.

The peace has gone, now danger looms,
Does the 'Old Man' know what waits?
Once called 'The Beast that ne'er forgets',
He must remember how man hates.

Remembers how his wife was killed,
How her tusks from her were sawn.
Remembers how his sons were kidnapped,
In circus ring they now perform.

What is there now for him to live for?
He's now too old to start again.
He must go on and try to bear
The constant threat of men.

Adam Thorp (15)
Sherborne, Dorset

shetland

The bird is tired.
Too tired to move.
Its last drop of strength has
dripped away in its mad escape
from the swamp-like sea.
On the tar-covered sand
a seal is wriggling
like a worm chopped in half.
The waves are hitting
a half-dead shoal of fish
that flap wildly
to get free of their
dark prison. Their tomb.
In Stourport, a man turns off
the engine of his car, walks into a
garage,
and buys two litres of Castrol oil.

Morgan Price (14)
Stourport High School
Stourport-on-Severn, Worcestershire

Owl

An owl is looking for food in the cold and misty night;
It cannot find anything but frosted grass.
He has a lovely furry face and wings like soft white hands.

Elizabeth Sims (7)
Combs Ford CP School
Stowmarket, Suffolk

Owl

The teddy bear sits patiently,
Left alone in the woods,
Forgotten
At night.
He preens himself,
As teddy bears do.
Stuffing
Falls.

The lighthouse swings its searching
Beams of vision, out
Across the sea of darkness.
Watching and waiting,
Motionless

As every tiny movement –
The waves and ripples in the dark ocean –
is silently observed.

Then the shrapnel falls:

The tiger pounces;
Claws and teeth, gleaming
In the moonlight.
They sink
Into the little parcel of flesh

And the dead mouse rises.

Ruth Hite (14)
Maharishi School
Ormskirk, Lancashire
(Roald Dahl Wondercrump School Award)

A Swan is on the Water

A swan is on the water;
It looks like another swan is stuck to its feet under water.
It is daytime, so the sun can make another swan.
Then, the wind ripples the water
And the reflection is wavy.
Straight lines of grasses at the edge
Are crinkly lines in the mirror of the water;
But it wasn't always like that . . .

Cans and bottles floated on brown sludge,
Nothing could live there,
A black slime on the surface of the water,
And nobody cared.

But now, someone does care,
The pond is clean,
Ducks nest around its grassy edges,
And swans can paddle around
And look at their faces in the water.

Rhys Grant (7)
Combs Ford CP School
Stowmarket, Suffolk

Fish Talk

'Oi, fish face, your move,' said the Shubunkin to the Koi
'Prawn to Koi four,' came the fishy reply.
'Ah ha, beat that you Sprat.'
'Why are they playing chess?' asked a puzzled Tench.
'Don't you know,' said the Sturgeon before he went on his
　　rounds.
'In today's Daily Scale it says that the Grand Master
　　Carparov is coming in by Flying Fish today.'
'If I move my Seahorse here,' said the Shubunkin.
'Oh no, I fell for that hook, line and sinker,' said the Koi.
'Codswallop you almost made me sacrifice my Bream!'
'Don't make waves!'
'This game has turned into a scalemate,
How about a game of pool?'

Jonathan Napier (11)
Mowden School
Hove, East Sussex
(Age Category Winner)
(School of the Year)

shark

Shark, Moves through the water
Graceful like geese in flight.
Vicious jaws are gaping wide.
The jaws of death. Waiting.

Sleek. Hydrodynamic.
Built to be the hunter.
Ultimate predator,
With a killing instinct.

The shark is submerged. A
Submarine for battle.
Armed. Weaponry that
Kills and ravages the weak.

A fisherman is waiting.
The bait is ready. As it
Hangs in the water, a
Reel screams. The shark is caught.

Hunter being hunted . . .

Peter Bourne (14)
Stourport High School
Stourport-on-Severn, Worcestershire

WORLD TORN APART

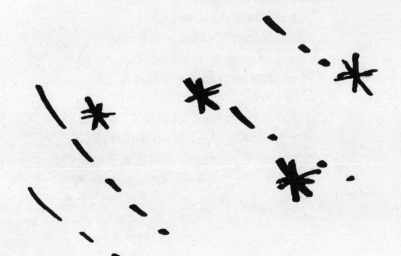

The Collector

I am a collector.
Not just stamps and stickers,
Books and Barbies,
Bits of glittery rock.
In my mind I store all sorts of things:
Whispers from the playground,
Games we'll play at lunch time,
The pattern of the pavement,
Reflections from the mirror.
Other pictures stay locked in me:
The faces of the hungry,
The ruins of bombed houses,
Dirty, crowded hospitals,
The way they chop down forests.
I don't choose to collect these things.
They just jump into my mind.

Ellen Coffey (7)
Handford Hall CP
Ipswich, Suffolk
(Age Category Winner)

Osaka, January 1995

In the Japanese town of Osaka
on top of what remains of a once happy home
stands a sad little boy.
His face wet with tears and
This thumb in his mouth,
the boy clutches onto his last possession –
a tattered teddy bear.
Lumps of concrete lie, hurled
from rooftops by a giant's hand.
The flimsy wooden walls collapsed easily
and now lie splintered among the rubble.
The boy points downwards and pleads
for passers-by to rescue his Mother
who is buried deep below the wreckage.
They hear his cries but do not stop.
Their own lives destroyed, they walk on by.
The boy holds tightly onto his threadbare friend.
His home shaken to pieces.
His world torn apart.

Nicola Vaughan (14)
The Gregg School
Southampton, Hampshire

Quake

The earth is rearranging her plates
in preparation
for her latest meal.
She opens her jagged mouth and selects
the choicest morsels of
human flesh
to dine upon.
Above in the city
people are screaming;
crying for help that will be
long in coming.
Buildings are swaying
like blades of grass
in a macabre dance.
The city is cracking up.
People are falling
into dark crevices
to satisfy the earth's cavernous hunger.
She savours the essence of
fear.
Death hangs in the air
and lies below with the broken bodies
in ready-made graves.
The earth sighs with relief.
A few thousand souls and she will be appeased.
A sea of flames
is lapping at the edge of people's panic.

They wait in terror.
A city falls.

Rebecca Richardson (14)
The Gregg School
Southampton, Hampshire
(Age Category Winner)

Coca Cola and Guns

Born of war a young child weeps,
Surrounded by army jeeps Coca Cola and guns,
Smuggled out under camouflaged canopies,
To a safe place,
So safe it was bombed,
Her spirit was killed,
But her body lived on,
An empty shell crawling,
Begging,
Slowly dying,
Turned away by the people of Coca Cola and guns,
Made to die in a cruel land drenched in blood,
While the people of Coca Cola and guns are borne away in
false helicopters,
Home to their false paradise,
Far far away.

Ralph Simmonds (10)
Mayflower CP School
Harwich, Essex

War Report

I see war every day,
An image,
A concept,

On a screen.

Third-hand information.

It's a war caged by glass,
Boxed by technology.

Another bomb on a bus
A maimed man, slumped over the steering wheel.

More blood.
The reporter sees it
I see it
The world sees it

Live death.

It's a daily conflict.
Tune in for the next episode,
A massacre framed by mobile phones and sports cars.

The duplication of death,
Part of the daily routine.

Eleanor Lloyd (15)
Carnforth, Lancashire

Kamikaze

Blood-spoilt sheets.
Once white. Now red.
They flap as if they were wings of the doves of peace.
So far away, so close to home.

Twisted metal hides the bloody carnage of when cold steel
    meets cold steel.
What once was perfect is now broken.
Bodies, reared by careful mothers, lie battered and
    unrecognizable.

Why do you come Kamikaze?
Because you were the best. That is why you come.

Reared by careful mothers, chosen to die by fearful fathers.
For it is honourable to die in battle.
Not to return is considered good. That is why you come.

Perfect bodies, reared by careful mothers, now lie, staining
    the deck.
When moulded steel meets a moulded body.
Only destruction occurs.

Now you lie under a blood-spoilt sheet, with the men you
were told to hate, staining the deck.

Helen Hadley (15)
The Duchess's High School
Alnwick, Northumberland

The Defeat of Chechenya

The presidential palace
Of Grozney is burning,
Burning away the resistance,
Symbolising the defeat
Of Chechenya.
Blood
Is running in rivulets down the rubble-covered street.
People are running,
Their faces are so begrimed
That no skin can be seen.
But their eyes have no shields
To stop the naked fear and terror
From being unleashed
Or to stop them witnessing
The defeat of Chechenya.
The picture is alight
With flames pouring
From shattered jewels
That once were windows,
That once had reflected the sun in all its glory.
But the sun is no longer shining
Upon the City of Hell,

The only things that shine in the light of exploding shells,
Are tears.
The defeat of Chechenya has killed
The last glimmer
Of hope.

Kirstine Haslehurst (15)
The Gregg School
Southampton, Hampshire

A Ghost Among the Dead

I wander the body-strewn battlefield, choking on thick
   acrid smoke,
The memories flooding back of the previous day's horrors,
If only they didn't.
I remember the cracks and bangs of rifle and cannon,
A ring of ragged corpses around the regiment's fallen
colours,
If only they'd survived.
I come upon the blood-red ridge, stained by the deaths of
   the innocent,
One body stands out from the mass of tangled limbs,
If only I hadn't gone to look.
My body, my face twisted in a gruesome expression of pain,
The sabre that had been my doom glints cruelly in my
   stomach,
If only it had been quick.
And now I begin to remember my final living moments,
And I think back to that fateful hour,
If only I hadn't been there.
My regiment caught in open ground,
By the thunder of hooves as the Dragoons closed in,
If only I'd run.
Rifle flints not sparking in the misty air,
As the sabres flashed down from above, signalling my
   death,
If only I'd escaped.
I now stand and think, and survey the devastated scene
   before me,

All the blood, the bodies, the ruined lives of so many,
If only there had not been a battle.
Was it really worth all the killing?
Did so many die for nothing?
If only I hadn't been killed, doomed to wander between
    realities as a soul
in torment for the rest of eternity.
A ghost among the dead.

Peter Haswell (15)
St Leonard's RC Comprehensive
Durham, County Durham

This One should Know

This one should know what we give of his life,
So tell him some lies to flatten his fear,
This one should know how we're twisting the knife,
So never let on if his time is near.

Aren't they all strange his maddening views?
Why can't he see that he cannot win?
Has he not heard or read in the news –
Does he not know you're supposed to give in?

This one should learn the rules of his life,
No thoughts ever stay, no impact is made.
No one gets more than a child and a wife,
Dust flows to dust, and worth tends to fade.

Isn't he strange to ask for some more?
Why can't he see that he is so small?
Silence his whines and return to the floor,
As his heirs start to doubt he existed at all.

Miles Trent (16)
Kettering, Northamptonshire

PUDDLES
ABOUT

Rain

The lights are all on, though it's just past midday,
There are no more indoor games we can play,
No one can think of anything to say,
It rained all yesterday, it's raining today,
It's grey outside, inside me it's grey.

I stare out of the window, fist under my chin,
The gutter leak drips on the lid of the dustbin,
When they say, cheer up, I manage a grin,
I draw a fish on the glass with a sail-sized fin,
It's sodden outside, and it's damp within.

Matches, bubbles and paper pour into the drains,
Clouds smother the sad laments from the trains,
Grandad says it brings on his rheumatic pains,
The moisture's got right inside my brains,
It's raining outside, inside me it rains.

Elizabeth Jones (7)
Our Lady Immaculate Primary School
Chelmsford, Essex

The Storm

Cunning clouds billowed across the sky
Like an enormous gloomy-grey squadron,
Carrying huge water bombs,
Which exploded,
Scattering their wet debris,
Drowning and drenching.
The driving rain
Stamped on the roof,
Banging and beating,
And bounced to the ground.
Bigger, bolder, bleaker clouds
Crowded in and crushed the sky,
Creating an inky-black curtain,
Which stretched as far as the eye could see,
And was broken only
By a sudden streak
Of forked, fluorescent lightning.

Nisha Anil Doshi (9)
Acomb, Yorkshire

Looking Out

Suspended and serene, our room was sweet with sleep.
Explosion: iron-fisted thunder slams the glass.
That first eclipse of lightning punched open my eyes,
exorcised spirits of bedroom objects
(hurling their shadowy souls against the walls).
I rushed onto the balcony;
another thunderous heartburst sent me dancing back inside
and you laughed.

In the vacant arena of sky, behind screens of torn-down
cloud,
the storm manufactured its steel dustbins,
the white-hot sparks of its industry sending a crazy caravan
of silhouettes across the room.
Faceless houses paid no attention to frothy
Spears of electricity stalking fields in a broken-backed
waltz.
You sat in bed, face cupped in the flower of your hands,
and muttered your remarks across the strobe-lit emptiness.

A brief absence of noise, the show flickered wordlessly on;
then
with the clash of pages in steel books
the rain draped down.
I edged back, and the twinkling beard
only pebbled my toes.

Your fear was
in the dropped stitch of your speech,
the way the dark diamonds of your eyes
drank in the startled room,
your measured, 'Staying up much longer?'

'Yeah, a while. Good night.'
Silence from you who wouldn't close the verbal contract;
I signed off, released you with,
'Sleep well, then.'

The storm sparked on against the cheap black-rubber sky,
taking brutal photographs of shaggy hills.
And still, the cold steam of pulverised water veiling
my skin, the rhythmed draughts of your breath
at my back, and me keeping watch.

Eva Okwonga (17)
West Drayton, Middlesex
(Age Category Winner)

The Storm at Sea

Sailors slipping
Boat rocking
Boat out of control
Black clouds
Lightning coming
Boat creaking
Men terrified
Boat breaking
Man overboard
Waves crashing
Sailors screaming
Swimming to land.

Daniel Killeen (6)
Grange Infant School
Daventry, Northants

The Wind Howls His Answer

The sky is a picture of darkness
while icy air sends a message
of numbness around my body.
Dying leaves design a winter cake
with bitter snow as lemon icing
as my feet like teeth
crunch into its frozen decorations.

Silence echoes through the bare trees,
Lights sparkle like cats' eyes,
houses are windbreakers
protecting their owners from the cutting air.

While I wander through the swaying trees
my dog departs over the shivering grass;
his bark bites through the living night.
I call his name;
the wind howls his answer.

Richard Allchild (11)
Mowden School
Hove, East Sussex
(School of the Year)

Stormy Sea

Roaring, splashing
dancing white pumas
on the surface of the water
swirling whirlpool
going round and round
white pumas
crashing on grey rocks
crash crashing
lightning flashing
The storm is at its end.

Lucy Hockham (8)
Milford-on-Sea Primary School
Milford-on-Sea, Hampshire

The Snow

The snow falls from the sky
Like pretty patterns.
It's like fluffy cotton wool.
It's soft and cuddly.

The sun is sparkling off the river
Like drops of rain.
It looks pretty on nice days.
It's like sparkling gold.

The storm is like a roaring bear.
It makes you frightened.
You get scared.
There's a lot of rain.
The wind is hard.

The rain drips off branches.
It's drizzly.
There are puddles about.
It's wet and damp.

The wind is cold.
It makes your cheeks red.
It blows hard.
It blows trees over.
It blows you over.

The clouds look like wool from sheep.
They look like animals in the sky.

Lauren Westmore (5)
Hilperton CE Primary School
Trowbridge, Wiltshire

Winter Is

Stars cracking in the sky, falling from space.
Tractors sprinkling salt on slippery roads,
Feathery patterns on car windows
Freezing my hands as I wipe a space,
Hot sweaty clothes scratching my body,
Snow, a rich soft jacket on the garden,
Baubles on my Christmas tree.

Toni Mott (6)
Handford Hall
Ipswich, Norfolk
(Age Category Winner)

Autumn

Conkers, conkers
Drive me bonkers.
Rain, rain
Is a pain.
Autumn breezes
Give me sneezes.
I wish it was
Summer again.

Jack Ring (6)
Belleville Primary School
Battersea, London

My Place

My place is hot like a burning oven at the
warmest time
When the sun rises.
But the best time is when the moon comes
out,
it is nice and cold like an ocean.
(It is India)

Kalpesh Chauhan (10)
Barham Primary School
Wembley, Middlesex

Beach

The apricot sun sets
into a watery quilt,
The palm trees stand
like men on stilts.

The sea is a carnival
that dances to a steel band,
The tropical sun
is a faraway land.

Nazmin Khan (12)
Westbourne High School
Ipswich, Suffolk

Shallow Waters

In Weymouth,
The clear sea,
Is glowing,
You can go out,
Three miles,
But still,
The sea,
Is only at your knee.

Hayley Gray (9)
Townhill Junior School
Southampton, Hampshire

HE SHOWED US PICTURES

Faces in the street

There for a second,
Gone the next,
Thousands of faces –
An ocean of features.
Swirling, flowing,
Never repeating,
Always changing,
Heads bobbing,
Like seagulls.

Smiles gentle,
Frowns harsh,
Like waves.
A thousand stories,
Quickly disappearing,
Inviting me to read,
Tussocks of hair,
On a pavement moor.

Daniel Greenfield (13)
Simon Langton Grammar School for Boys
Canterbury, Kent

The Mind of a Wolf

Enter the mind of a wolf
Feel the cold, feel the chase,
Enter the mind of a wolf
Be the hunter, the midnight ace
Enter the mind of a wolf.

Enter the mind of a wolf
Use your legs, use your teeth
Enter the mind of a wolf
A killing machine underneath
Enter the mind of a wolf.

Enter the mind of a wolf
Gotta keep tough, keep growling
Enter the mind of a wolf
Ruthless and howling
Enter the mind of a wolf.

Enter the mind of a wolf
But this is not a *real* wolf
It is the wolf of mankind
It is stronger, it is greater
This is the wolf of the mind.

Stephen Van Riel (10)
The Rookeries Carleton J&I School
Pontefract, West Yorkshire

snake

Snake slides smoothly into his chair.
The plush leather contrasts with his waxy skin.
He slowly sends his lazy gaze gliding round the office,
searching,
but on the surface,
placid.

His eye catches
the bald pate of a jaded personnel manager
sitting at his desk,
rewriting the payrolls for the shop floor.

He slips to the floor,
slides over,
his Biro clicking.
Click, the manager hears the sound and realises its
significance ...
He tries to get out, to run,
but all around him are desks,
and he is too old and weary for a chase.

'Can we have a chat ...
I'm a bit worried about these proposed staff cuts?'
Though phrased as a question,
it's an order.
The serpent doesn't do requests.

The other staff realise what is going on.
They crouch together, hidden in a corner,
some wielding rulers and drawing boards
as a crude spear and shield arrangement.
They know it would be futile,
but it could give others time to escape
if the snake comes their way.

The manager is taken to the boardroom.
He says nothing, hypnotised by the snake.
His will is weak, and swiftly the snake bites him,
his fangs drenched in bitter-sweet venom,
sweet
as the manager will no longer have to fear the flicking
    tongue.

Slowly he sinks to the Axminster,
his breaths shallowing, until
nothing.

There is a cracking sound as the snake kneels by him,
his jaw dislocated.
With powerful tongue the corpse is shovelled into the
    snake's maw,
and digested.
All that remains is a slightly fatter executive,
and some out-of-date files.

James McLintock (14)
Wisbech, Cambridgeshire
(Age Category Winner)

Queen of the Iceni

Onward she rides,
Her hair streaming out behind her
The scars of battle enshrouding her
Yet she shows no
Agony or Fear.
Her savage army advances,
Driving terror into the hearts
Of the enemy.
Hear the yells of the horses and the clattering
Of the chariot's wheels
Hear the yells and screams
Of the Romans fleeing
No army has yet defied her
Strong is the tribe
Whose army is led by
Boudicca, Queen of the Iceni.

Laura Barnett (8)
Lewes, Sussex

Moving On

Sophisticated ladies in smart suits,
Balancing on slim heels,
Carrying Marks and Spencer meals,
Hurry past,
Heads down. Such a lot to do!
Boys rush by in Nike trainers,
Weaving their skateboards through the crowds.
No worries!
No cares!

Children pouring past,
School bags laden
Too much homework
Spoils their fun
Of switching on computers as soon as home is reached!

City executives push past now
Briefcases heavy
Deadlines to meet
Success makes them too tired for conversation!

Everyone rushing,
Everyone moving,
Makes old Mary dizzy to watch
from her home; a cardboard box,
On platform nine.

Joanne Hughes (12)
St Aloysius College
Glasgow

Photographer at the Parthenon

In the heat of the afternoon sun,
At the bottom of the hill that leads up to the Parthenon,
We stood, smiling into a camera
Almost as old as the person behind it.
Triumphant, he emerged from the cloak.
He wore a black bowler hat,
A natty pinstriped waistcoat
And clumsy clown shoes.
He was bald,
His head was wrinkly like a prune.
His eyes were watery brown;
He had a few teeth missing.
We talked for a while.
Proudly, he showed us pictures of his son's wedding.
He seemed sad and lonely.
Just before we left,
Into my hand he thrust a shiny coin,
To remember him by.
As we left, I clutched the coin
And thought of the poor old man
In the heat,
Taking photos,
Freezing the moments of time which fly so fast.

Jessica Huth (12)
Port Regis School,
Shaftesbury, Dorset
(Age Category Winner)

God Deals the Cards, You Play the Hand

Glum, depressed, sorry for myself.
It's work experience week
What have I got? A Special Needs school
What? Kim's with an actress
I'm with a freak.

Glum, depressed, ashamed of myself.
Gemma she's no freak.
Blue eyes, a funny grin,
Blonde curls and dribble on her chin.
Sweet-tempered with button nose and cheeks.

Sunny, cheerful, full of herself.
I'm the one who's out of place
God deals the cards, she plays her hand
Which is one short of ace,
But it's not lost, just misplaced.

Sunny, cheerful, *proud* of myself
From my 'Gemma experience place'
God deals the cards, I've played my hand.
Grateful to her, remembering her face.
I think again. Who wins the race?

Charity Garnett (13)
City of London Girls' School
Barbican, London

Bright City Nightlife

Girls and boys come out to play
Lured by the glitz of stolen flyers

They burst, glittering upon the stiff
Nylon streets

Scorning the culture houses, like
moths to the flame they are drawn
to the heaving clubs.

Caffeine and saccharine buzz in
the plastic cafes

Neon lights are exchanged for parental
pay-packets

As shiny unhappy people bomb themselves
in search of pleasure

Eleanor Ferguson (14)
Varndean School
Brighton, East Sussex

The Poacher's Gifts

First . . . the way the moon prances,
From the dew on the grass,

To the spider's web,
To the icy cold barrel
Of my gun,
And back again,
Continuously,
As if in a ballet.
And second,
The speed and grace
Of the hare,
And his movement
As he strides,
Leaps and bounds
Into his full-flight run.
Leaves fall,
Gently,
Like the silent swoop
Of the owl . . .
Which is my third gift.
And my last but not least,
Which only old poachers can give,
Is the art of becoming a ghost,
In tune with the dark,
And in love with the wild.
But always in time for breakfast.

Gordon Cullingford (12)
Halesworth Middle School
Halesworth, Suffolk
(Age Category Winner)

Fly

He stood on the lonely cliff,
He could fly.
What did he have to live for?
What could he do?
He had no friends,
No family,
He could fly,
He knew he could fly.

He stood on the lonely step,
He could fly.
What did he have to live for?
Nobody loved him,
Nobody wanted him,
He knew he could fly.
What could he do?
He flew.

Katie Moore (11)
Ormskirk LED School
Ormskirk, Lancashire

The Tabernacle

The Minister adjusts his specs,
His Audience shivers,
The air is dead.

He begins,
Allegro, Crescendo,
Walloping out words.
Until he hits his hwyl.
The amplitude increases,
Each word accentuated,
Every syllable enunciated.
He thumps the pulpit,
Shattering his gesturing glasses.
OAPs and Grandchildren sit enthralled
Warned of the dangers of:
Alcohol, Bars, Crime,
Vandals, Wanton Women.
He hits his high,
The cross reverberates,
The mice shudder,
The organist weeps.
He reaches the pinnacle.
He loves God.
God speaks through him.
Then it is over,
The crowd wipe their brows,
Leave on a spiritual high,
Determined to convert Porthcawl,
Not with the sword,
But by coffee mornings and jumble sales.

Stephen John (16)
Porthcawl Comprehensive School
Porthcawl, Mid Glamorgan
(Age Category Winner)

Sixty

Sixty, the big six O, six zero,
When you're sixty, you're definitely old.
No matter how fit you are.
Congratulations.
You take retirement,
Finally settle down in that little house on the coast
That you always had your eye on.
And then you have time.
What do you do?
You can't suffer a mid-life crisis, you're too old for that,
Now that you're sixty.

Why not go to Bingo?
You go to Bingo.
You look at the other people there and ask yourself a
question;
Should I be here?
This is for old people!
Oh, you forgot, you're over the hill, way past it,
Now that you're sixty.

Too much time.
Too little to do.
You wonder.
You have time to think.

In the Bingo hall, a lady in her forties comes over to your
    table.
'Are you all right, dear?'
You're an old dear,
Now that you're sixty.

So you moan about the weather
The cold
The Council
The youth of today
The good old days.
Nobody listens.
You wish the lady would come again and talk to you.
You wish anybody would come and talk.
Anybody.
But they don't.

Peter Bonnington (16)
Simon Langton Boys' School
Canterbury, Kent

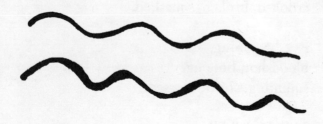

Old People

Old people ...
  Their faces are like a crinkled chip.
  Their faces explode with laughter,
  All gummy mouths and floppy cheeks.

Old people ...
  They're great in their way.
  And if you look closely in their eyes
  You can see a young little face.

Stephen Beresford (10)
Laleham C of E Primary School
Laleham, Middlesex

Faces

Nostrils dripping,
noses sniffing,
crooked, broken, squashed.

Eyes drooping,
bloodshot, bulging,
squinting, shifty, crossed.

Mouths dribbling,
false teeth clicking,
lips chapped and cracked.

Eyebrows hairy,
caterpillar-furry,
spiky, knitted, thatched.

Cheeks flabby,
blotched, baggy,
broken veins and boils.

Ear crinkled,
cauliflower-crumpled,
wind breaks, aerofoils.

Chins wobbly,
dimpled, knobbly,
stubbly brillo pads.
Skin wrinkled,
zits and pimples,
cold sores, warts and scabs.

Daniel Korachi (12)
Simon Langton Boys' School
Canterbury, Kent

Going Back

The large, heavy door opens.
It is dark inside, but the light shines through.
It's familiar, though I feel I don't know it.

It's all coming back now; the red carpet, polished floor, the
hat stand.
Everything is smaller, not so huge and frightening as I
    remember,
The flowers at the side, exactly the same, meticulously
    arranged.

I notice the pictures on the walls. Every detail has
    remained.
Smart women in fine clothing, gentlemen in uniform.
Now they are just paintings. Before, they were real.

This room is empty now. Something is missing.
Soon it will all disappear and be forgotten.
Soon the small flowers that gave it life will die.

She cannot care for them any longer.
She is not here.

Charlotte Foster (16)
The Holy Trinity School
Crawley, West Sussex

LAST WORD

A Poet's Problems

You're told to write a poem,
About anything at all,
You don't know what to write about,
You're feeling quite a fool.
If only they had suggested
Things like cauldrons, witches, warts,
Friendships, food or fashion,
It would concentrate my thoughts.
I wish I could decide right now,
I've got the world to choose from.
I feel confused, my brain is dead,
Roald Dahl would have no problem.
I'll never be a Roald Dahl,
He was just too clever,
He got inside all children's minds,
THE GREATEST WRITER EVER.

Jo Harris (11)
George Abbot School
Guildford, Surrey

Index of Titles

Index of Poets